Cultivating Innovation

Cultivating Innovation

Transforming Organizations by Empowering People and Culture

YUL WILLIAMS

Cultivating Innovation
Transforming Organizations by Empowering People and Culture

ISBN: 978-1-78324-360-0 (paperback)
ISBN: 978-1-78324-363-1 (ebook)

Design and published by wordzworth.com

To my father, Henry Williams, Jr. (1925–2007),
and my mother, Claudia Baxter Williams
— for two lifetimes of inspiration.

Foreword

n today's rapidly evolving business landscape, innovation is no longer a luxury—it's a necessity for survival and growth. Yet, many organizations struggle to foster a true culture of innovation, often focusing on processes and technologies while overlooking their most valuable asset: their people.

In "Cultivating Innovation: Transforming Organizations by Empowering People and Culture," Dr. Yul Williams offers a refreshing and much-needed perspective on organizational innovation. Drawing from his extensive experience in national security, cybersecurity, and academia, he presents a compelling case for placing people at the heart of innovation efforts.

What sets this book apart is its holistic approach to innovation. Dr. Williams doesn't just provide insights on innovation tools or techniques; he offers a comprehensive framework for transforming entire organizations. From fostering an innovation mindset to implementing effective idea management systems, from encouraging cross-functional collaboration to balancing centralized and decentralized decision-making, this book covers all aspects of building and sustaining an innovation culture.

One of the book's greatest strengths is its emphasis on practical implementation. Dr. Williams doesn't just tell us what to do; he shows us how to do it, offering concrete strategies and real-world examples that readers can apply in their own organizations. His insights on overcoming mental barriers to innovation, developing innovation champions, and ensuring long-term commitment to innovation are particularly valuable.

As someone who has spent years studying and promoting innovation, I found myself nodding in agreement throughout this book. Dr. Williams' ideas resonate with my own experiences and observations, yet he also offers fresh perspectives that challenge conventional thinking about innovation.

Whether you're a senior executive looking to drive organizational change, a manager seeking to foster innovation within your team, or an individual contributor wanting to unleash your creative potential, you'll find valuable insights in these pages. This book is not just about making organizations more innovative; it's about creating workplaces where people can thrive, grow, and contribute their best ideas.

In a world where change is the only constant, the ability to innovate continuously is perhaps the most important competency any organization can develop. "Cultivating Innovation" provides a roadmap for developing this competency, not through top-down mandates or flashy innovation labs, but by unleashing the creative potential of every individual in the organization.

I wholeheartedly recommend this book to anyone interested in driving innovation and creating more dynamic, adaptive, and successful organizations. Dr. Williams has made a significant contribution to the field of innovation management, and I believe his ideas will shape how we think about and practice innovation for years to come.

Erica Dobbs

Founder and Chief Executive Officer, Dobbs Defense Solutions, LLC

Preface

The topic of innovation is pervasive. As new technologies appear, they change the way people and organizations live, work and play. In general, these changes are necessary to progress forward. While innovation is the catalyst for change, there are a plethora of methodologies and processes from which to choose to advance an idea as a possible solution for a pressing problem, an innovation.

While the means of creating the next big innovation is important, many of the descriptions of the various methodologies and processes for transforming ideas into innovations uniformly ignore the core consideration that make innovations possible, the people. People drive the processes by putting forth the ideas, effort of championing the ideas through the stages of the chosen processes and transforming themselves and their respective organizations into innovation powerhouses.

Within the realm of innovation, people are required to be bold, think outside the box, collaborate with peers and leaders alike. They must understand how to interpret negative comments about their respective ideas and change the minds of the naysayers. They must possess a drive to succeed but not be broken by failure along the path. They must seek opinions and welcome participation from the most diverse people they can engage. They must be organized and ready to take on the world to give their idea the best possible chance to thrive as a potential innovation. Where are these people? Great question.

The people with these characteristics work in traditional hierarchical (private, public, military and academic) organizations but are constrained in their thinking and actions by the roles they are assigned. The leaders, managers and workers all fit this description, and this is likely codified within the organization's business plan. No innovation is likely to occur in such environment's because every thought and action is prescribed. So, if the organization is to be transformed into an innovation powerhouse, it must first transform its people.

All the previously identified characteristics of innovative people can be taught and reinforced to the people who are already familiar with the business. While the transformation will take time, as people get excited about the possibilities of playing key roles that contribute to the success of the business an innovative culture will emerge and grow into one that values people, their contributions and the success of the business. The people described as virtual unicorns of innovation exist as employees (at all levels) of existing organizations.

This book is meant to provide insights and a bit of guidance to help hierarchical organizations to transform themselves to dominate in a hyper-competitive environment. The content is helpful to leaders, managers and workers who want to learn how to break out of the hierarchical mindset and begin to think, act and thrive as an innovation powerhouse. The transformation being touted is focused internally to the business entity but embodies principles that are valid beyond the walls of any given organizational entity. As the innovation culture takes root, the business will experience employees who are more considerate of their fellow leaders, managers and peers. The business will experience greater diversity of product and service offerings and greater success and an organization that attracts and retains top talent to increase its long-term viability in its chosen market.

The content was written in a manner that avoids overly complicated terminology so the reader can easily grasp and adapt and apply the concepts in their respective work environments. No reader is expected to become an expert in building innovation cultures within their respective organizations after completing this book, but they will be acutely aware of issues to be encountered and so practical approaches to lighten the cognitive load and stress of going through the process.

Acknowledgements

Writing a book can be an intimidating, daunting and arduous undertaking if it is done in isolation. Fortunately, I routinely leaned on family, friends and professionals who provided me with the strength, motivation and uninhibited verbal feedback. For these experiences, I am forever grateful.

Foremost, I want to thank my wonderful wife Felecia, who gave me the space and encouragement to pursue this project. Likewise, to my two sons Justin and Joel, I want to thank them for the ridicule and constructive insights to ensure the content of the book was relevant.

Next, I want to thank my friends and principal editors, Vanee' Vines and Mabelean Simmons for their candid advice and feedback on all facets of the writing and layout. Their advice and counsel were critical in framing the information for the intended audience.

Furthermore, I want to thank the reviewers who suffered through untold manuscript versions. I appreciate you all. Reviewers included Vernessa Alexander, Steven Cook, JB Bryan, Clarence Jones Jr., Dr. Loretta Cheeks, Timothy Teal, Sarah Armstead, Joseph Patrick, Sheila Bent, Michael Bent, Ashley Staten, George Bivens, Dr. Latoshka Castle, Ayinde Stewart, Traci Gosnell, Bianca

McNair, Robert Barksdale, Beth Lange and Perry Taylor. Thank you all for your tremendous feedback and patience.

Additionally, I want to thank a great friend and national security expert, Ms. Erica Dobbs, for the book's forward. Thank you for sharing your outstanding insights.

As mentioned earlier, composing this work from the content perspective was the simplest of the numerous tasks, but the village of experts, friends and contributors made it all possible.

Thanks to you all.

Contents

Introduction and Background

In today's rapidly evolving and highly competitive business landscape, innovation has become a critical factor for organizations to survive, thrive, and maintain a competitive edge. The importance of innovation can be attributed to numerous factors.

Staying ahead of the curve, for instance, is an important factor to consider. Companies that consistently innovate are better equipped to anticipate and adapt to changing market conditions, customer needs, and technological advancements. Embracing innovation enables organizations to stay ahead of their competitors and position themselves as industry leaders. Innovation has turned into the buzzword of the day, so organizations do not want to be left in dust when it comes to being competitive. More organizations are taking advantage of innovations as the means to remain viable and to compete into today's rapidly advancing market.

While companies are jumping into innovation, they should always consider their goals of meeting customer expectations. Organizations can innovate to their heart's desire but if the results do nothing to meet or exceed customer expectations, it adds no real value to the organization's ability to compete. Innovation allows companies to develop new products, services, and solutions that address evolving customer needs and preferences. Continuously improving and expanding their offerings facilitates organizations in delivering enhanced value to their customers, fostering loyalty and driving growth.

Many sources of information discuss innovation methodologies focused on product development that is externally focused. While this is ultimately the desired outcome, to get there, the internal innovation mindset, practices, and organizational culture are key elements to improving organizational efficiency and productivity. Innovation is not limited to products and services; it also encompasses processes, systems, and business models. When organizations choose to innovate in these areas, they can streamline operations, reduce costs, and improve overall efficiency and productivity, there gaining a competitive advantage.

Attracting and retaining talent is one of the best ways to infuse new life into the organization. If organizations are exceptional in retaining existing talent but have not excelled at attracting new talent, the organization's long-term viability may be in jeopardy. Innovative companies tend to attract and retain top talent, as creative and skilled individuals are drawn to organizations that foster a culture of innovation and provide opportunities for growth and development. This, in turn, strengthens the company's human capital and enhances its ability to innovate further.

Fostering agility and resilience is a great way to ensure that the organization and its workforce are working with open minds. As the business environment is continually disrupted by innovations introduced by competitors, each organization must avoid being perennially locked into a static mindset. (Kuratko, Goldsby and Hornsby, 2018) In an uncertain and rapidly changing business environment, innovation enables organizations to be more agile and responsive to market disruptions, technological shifts, and evolving customer demands. Innovative companies are better equipped to navigate challenges and emerge stronger.

Remember that innovation is a critical driver of organizational success in today's competitive landscape. Companies that prioritize and invest in innovation are better positioned to adapt to change, deliver superior customer value, improve operational efficiency, attract top talent, drive long-term growth, and build resilience in the face of uncertainty.

There are several common elements shared by popular innovation methodologies such as Design Thinking, Incubation, Lean Startup, and Agile. While no particular methodology was selected as the basis for the offered insights, organizations may feel free to select the methodologies that are best suited to satisfying their respective goals. Even though numerous methodologies are being used by organizations now, please note that when examined at a high level, they share a great number of commonalities. Some of the commonalities among modern innovation methodologies include:

Customer-centricity: All four selected methodologies emphasize the importance of understanding and addressing customer needs and desires. Design Thinking focuses on empathy and user-centered design, while Lean Startup and Agile prioritize customer feedback and iterative development based on user input. Incubation also considers market demand and customer validation (Hughes, Chapnick, Block and Saptak, 2021).

Iterative process: Each methodology follows an iterative approach, allowing for continuous improvement and refinement of ideas or products. Design Thinking has an iterative process of prototyping and testing, Lean Startup uses the build-measure-learn feedback loop, Agile relies on short development cycles called sprints, and Incubation involves ongoing mentoring and adaptation (Ivanova, Lee and Jane, 2024).

Experimentation and learning: All methodologies encourage experimentation, prototyping, and learning from failures. Design Thinking promotes rapid prototyping, Lean Startup emphasizes validated learning, Agile supports learning through regular reviews and retrospectives, and Incubation provides a safe space for testing and refining ideas. Learning by developing experimentation skills is an effective way to increase student motivation and involvement in the science or science learning process (Ratnaningtyas, D.I,. & Wilujeng: 2021). Such an approach is applicable to the motivation and learning of innovation learning process.

Collaboration and cross-functional teams: Each methodology recognizes the value of collaboration and diverse perspectives. Design Thinking encourages multidisciplinary teams, Lean Startup often involves close collaboration between different functions, Agile relies on self-organizing and cross-functional teams, and Incubation provides access to a network of mentors and experts. Cross-functional team constructs promote high-quality interactions between representatives from various functional elements within an enterprise that has a direct effect on factors such as creativity, product development lifecycles and cost (Jassawalla and Sashittal, 2006).

Flexibility and adaptability: These methodologies promote flexibility and the ability to pivot or adapt based on new insights or changing circumstances. In addition to the specific innovation methodologies, however, other facets of the enterprise must be engaged for the organization to realize positive outcomes (Sellar, and Anthonypillai, 2023). Design Thinking allows for the refinement of problem statements and solutions, Lean Startup supports pivoting based on market feedback, Agile enables teams to adjust priorities and requirements, and Incubation provides resources and support for adapting business models.

While each methodology has its unique features and areas of focus, these common elements contribute to their effectiveness in fostering innovation, reducing risk, and creating value for customers and stakeholders. As a key takeaway, these common elements also hint that nearly all of the methodologies embodying these elements may offer the necessary features needed to enable innovation activities no matter to the topic. Armed with such knowledge, the selection of a methodology for a business entity becomes less mentally taxing. The major decision point can be focused instead on how well the selected methodology aligns with the organizational business practices.

Traditional innovation methodologies often face several limitations that can hinder an organization's potential to remain competitive in today's dynamic business environment due to their inherent rigidity. Some methodologies, for instance, offer no flexibility to adapt to the changing environment to which the organization is exposed or must operate within to be successful. So, selection of the proper methodologies must be done with consideration of how the organization operates. Adopting popular and well-used innovation methodologies out of the box can be used for reference understanding but the organization must modify the baseline of the methodology to achieve the desired levels of success.

Some innovation methodologies lack agility and are difficult to customize to suit the needs of the organization. Many traditional innovation approaches follow a linear, stage-gate process that can be slow and rigid. This lack of agility makes it difficult for organizations to quickly adapt to changing market conditions, customer needs, and technological advancements, potentially causing them to fall behind more nimble competitors. Another characteristic of innovation methodologies is their overemphasis on incremental improvements. Traditional innovation methodologies often focus on making incremental improvements to existing products, services, or processes. While incremental innovations are important, an overemphasis on this approach can lead to missed opportunities for disruptive or radical innovations that could potentially reshape the industry and provide a significant competitive advantage. Also, in many existing organizations, information and knowledge is siloed and the thinking and collaboration opportunities are not generally encouraged or supported. In many organizations, innovation is confined to specific departments or teams, such as Research and Development (R&D) or product development. This siloed approach can stifle creativity and limit the cross-pollination of ideas across the organization. Without effective collaboration and knowledge sharing, companies may struggle to develop truly innovative solutions.

When organizations have no familiarity with innovation, there may be an inherent resistance to change that manifest as risk aversion. If the organizational leadership is satisfied with the status quo, then the need to innovate does not make sense. Traditional corporate cultures often prioritize stability and predictability over experimentation and risk-taking (Ramirez, Rivero, Beltran, Alvarez and Ramirez, 2017). This risk-averse mindset can discourage employees from exploring unconventional ideas or challenging the status quo, ultimately hampering the organization's ability to innovate and stay ahead of the competition.

In some cases, the organization makes the innovation activity or the selected methodology the focus of attention and fails to align the innovation pursuits with the organizational goals. Such moves result in insufficient customer focus. So, the organization becomes super-efficient but produces results that do not satisfy customer needs. Some traditional innovation methodologies are more inward-looking, focusing on the company's capabilities and resources rather than the evolving needs and preferences of customers. Without a deep understanding of customer pain points, behaviors, and aspirations, organizations may develop innovations that fail to resonate with their target audience. One of the biggest concerns about organizations adopting and implementing popular innovation methodologies, however, is the lack of a holistic approach. Traditional innovation approaches often treat innovation as a discrete activity rather than an integral part of the organization's overall strategy and culture. This fragmented approach can lead to a lack of alignment between innovation initiatives and the company's broader goals, resulting in suboptimal outcomes and missed opportunities for synergy.

To overcome these limitations, organizations are increasingly adopting more agile, customer-centric, and holistic approaches to innovation. These may include design thinking, lean startup methodologies, open innovation, and the cultivation of an innovation-friendly culture that encourages experimentation, collaboration, and continuous learning. Organizations embracing these modern approaches can better position themselves to drive meaningful innovations and maintain a competitive edge in today's fast-paced business landscape (Fouejieu, 2023). While these methodologies are being used by many organizations, successful implementations allow for tweaking of the respective methodologies to service the needs of the organization.

A people-centric approach to organizational innovation is crucial for fostering a culture that encourages creativity, collaboration, and continuous improvement. Placing people at the heart of innovation efforts can help tap into the full potential of their human capital and drive meaningful, sustainable innovation. Here are some key reasons why a people-centric approach is essential:

Empowering employees (i.e., people) builds trust between the organizational leadership and the employees. A people-centric approach empowers employees at all levels to contribute ideas, challenge assumptions, and actively participate in the innovation process. Creating an environment where people feel valued, heard, and supported, organizations can unlock the creativity and problem-solving capabilities of their workforce, leading to a more innovative and engaged culture. Along the same line of thought, fostering psychological safety is another key area the organization must emphasize the shift in organizational philosophy that welcomes new ideas and creative thinking about how to solve problems. When employees feel safe to take risks, express unconventional ideas, and learn from failures, they are more likely to engage in these innovative behaviors more routinely. A people-centric approach prioritizes building trust, open communication, and a non-judgmental atmosphere that allows employees to experiment and grow.

Leveraging diversity and inclusion is a critical area of emphasis that enables an organization to tap into the thinking of all employees. A people-centric approach recognizes the value of including everyone in driving innovation. When organizations actively seek out and include diverse perspectives, experiences, and skill sets, organizations can generate a broader range of ideas, challenge groupthink, and develop more creative solutions to complex problems. Inclusive innovation practices ensure that all voices are heard and that innovations cater to the needs of diverse stakeholders. This approach also greatly advantages the organization's overall capability because new voices and participation means that results will be more diverse and consider a wider range of customer needs and expectations.

To expand an organization's knowledgebase throughout its enterprise, a requirement to promote cross-functional collaboration is essential. Innovation often thrives at the intersection of different disciplines and expertise. A people-centric approach breaks down silos and encourages collaboration across functions, departments, and hierarchies. Creating opportunities for cross-functional teams to work together, share knowledge, and co-create solutions can foster a more cohesive and innovative culture. Like the diversity and inclusion emphasis, the collaboration emphasis brings the entire workforce knowledge into play as the organization works to satisfy its business goals.

Continuous learning and development are critical when attempting to outpace competitors (Fonseca, Silva, Silva & Pereira, 2019). New ideas and technologies come into the market on a consistent basis. All levels of the organization's workforce must be aware of and know how to harness the new ideas and technologies for the benefit of the organization. A people-centric approach prioritizes the ongoing learning and development of employees. Investing in training, mentoring, and opportunities for growth, organizations can equip their workforce with the skills, mindsets, and tools needed to drive innovation. This commitment to continuous learning also helps attract and retain top talent who value personal and professional development.

Always remember to ensure innovation goals are aligned with the organization's goals. A people-centric approach ensures that innovation efforts align with the organization's purpose, values, and goals. Engaging employees in defining and pursuing a shared vision for innovation can create a sense of meaning and purpose that inspires and motivates the workforce. This alignment also helps ensure that innovations are not only commercially viable but also socially responsible and sustainable.

A people-centric approach to organizational innovation recognizes that people are the ultimate drivers of creativity, change, and growth. Empowering employees, fostering psychological safety, leveraging diversity, promoting collaboration, investing in continuous learning, and aligning innovation with purpose, helps to create a vibrant, adaptive, and innovative culture that positions them for long-term success in today's rapidly evolving business landscape.

Book Organization

This book is organized in five themed parts that place emphasis on major topics relating to the transformation of traditionally hierarchical organizations that are not leveraging innovation as a means to be competitive. The transformation occurs internally, starting with the people at all levels. If business entities make the decision to become more innovative and are willing to take the necessary steps to do so, they can use the insights and guidance offered within the book to get them started on their respective innovation journeys. The points of emphasis are organized into chapters that are grouped into the themed parts as follows:

Part I: Understanding the Innovation Mindset
Part II: Building an Innovation Culture
Part III: Empowering People for Innovation
Part IV: Driving Innovation through Organizational Structures
Part V: Measuring and Sustaining Innovation

Each of the parts contain chapters that address issues relating to the theme being explored. If the reader has familiarity with a particular theme, the reader may choose to skip over the part and engage the other part(s) of interest.

PART I

Understanding the Innovation Mindset

CHAPTER 1

Innovation and Organizational Success

"Innovation distinguishes between a leader and a follower."

—Steve Jobs

To foster a people-centric approach to innovation, it's crucial to define innovation in a way that resonates with employees at all levels and aligns with the organization's goals and values. An innovation culture should embody a mindset and encourage continuous progress rather than a one-time event in order to achieve a specific outcome. In fact, here is a definition that captures the essence of this perspective:

Definition: Innovation is the creative pursuit of new ideas to realize products and service solutions that create value for the adopting organization, its customers, and its stakeholders (Rogers, 2003).

This definition embodies a mindset that embraces curiosity, risk-taking, experimentation, learning, and collaboration to drive meaningful change and growth. The role of innovation in business success has numerous facets. Organizations with a strong innovation mindset are better equipped to identify and seize opportunities, differentiate themselves from competitors, and create new markets or disrupt existing ones. Continuously pushing the boundaries of what is possible enables innovative organizations to stay ahead of the curve and maintain a competitive edge.

An innovation mindset keeps organizations focused on understanding and anticipating customer needs, preferences, and behaviors. Continuously seeking ways to improve products, services, and experiences, helps innovative organizations to deliver superior value to customers, fostering loyalty, and driving growth. As the topic of innovation is explored, it will become clear that the topic is not limited to external offerings; it is also a major driver of internal processes, systems, and ways of working. An innovation mindset encourages people to challenge the status quo, identify inefficiencies, and develop creative solutions that streamline operations, reduce costs, and improve productivity. Additionally, organizations with a strong innovation mindset are more attractive to top talent who value creativity, learning, and impact. When fostering a culture that encourages experimentation, rewards innovative thinking, and provides opportunities for growth, organizations can realize success in attracting and retaining the best and brightest minds.

In today's fast-paced and uncertain business environment, the ability to adapt and respond to change is critical. An innovation mindset encourages the acceptance and embracement of change, pivot quickly when needed, and find creative solutions to emerging challenges. Adaptability and resilience are essential for long-term success and sustainability. An innovation mindset can also address social and environmental challenges. When focused on creating shared value for all stakeholders, organizations can develop meaningful solutions that drive business success and contribute to a more sustainable and equitable world becomes possible.

The organizational leadership is responsible for teaching members of the organization's workforce about innovation practices and their effects on the organization and its goals.

Learning organizations encourage people to continually expand their capacity to create meaningful outcomes, where new ideas and patterns of thinking are nurtured, and where people are creating, acquiring, and transferring knowledge, and at modifying the organization's behavior to reflect new knowledge and insights. (Achdiat, et. al., 2023) Learning begins with ideas. As ideas are pursued, new insights are gained, shared and the organization advances, accordingly.

To cultivate an innovation mindset, the essential prerequisite is an environment that encourages curiosity, experimentation, and learning. This involves provisioning of resources and the support for innovative initiatives, celebrating successes and failures, and modeling innovative behaviors themselves. Embedding innovation into an organization's foundational culture and empowering employees to think creatively and take calculated risks, the full potential of their human capital may be harnessed.

CHAPTER 2

Characteristics of an Innovative Mindset

"The true sign of intelligence is not knowledge but imagination."

—Albert Einstein

An innovative mindset is characterized by a set of beliefs, attitudes, and behaviors that enable individuals and business entities to generate and implement new ideas effectively. There are numerous important characteristics of an innovative mindset, and they will be explored to provide a high-level perspective on the expectations for people serving the innovation goals of an organization. In this chapter, the term "innovator" is used as a principal role, but it is meant to represent the mindset of all the people within the organization who participate in the innovation process, for the purposes of the discussion. Using this approach, the discussion is simplified because unique roles within the innovation space do not require definition or explanation in the context of the characteristics being amplified. As the discussion progresses, more specificity of roles, their definitions, and the levels at which they become important in building an innovation culture are explored.

Innovators inherently possess a strong sense of curiosity. Curiosity represents the drive for acquiring new knowledge and experiences that can motivate innovative pursuits (Pinar, Storme, Davila, and Myszkowski, 2016). They have a deep desire to learn, explore, and understand the world around them. They ask questions, challenge assumptions, and seek out new knowledge and perspectives to broaden their horizons and spark new ideas. They are motivated by the desire to realize a better means of accomplishing a task or satisfying an individual or corporate goal. The innovator's innate curiosity is a key factor in driving the innovator to think more deeply about an issue and potentially engage others to gain additional perspective and to judge, at a high level, whether the issue is worth pursuing further. The curiosity of innovators enables them to wonder if an idea has merit or if a practical solution to a pressing issue is possible. They also think about if solutions to problems can be realized with existing knowledge and technologies, or if potential solutions require new knowledge and technologies. Curiosity is the stage where innovators may be seen drawing out concept drafts on the back of napkins or creating a vision of the possibilities if their ideas were realized. This activity precedes any formalized documentation because the innovator is going through the "what-if" stage of thinking about an issue. Some innovation methodologies refer to this type of activity "ideation". It represents the initial formation of ideas and concepts that could evolve into spectacular innovations.

An innovative mindset is open to new possibilities, ideas, and approaches. Innovators are willing to consider different viewpoints, embrace ambiguity, and let go of preconceived notions. They are receptive to feedback and see value in diverse perspectives. Innovators must be open minded because ideas formulated on only their individual knowledge is limited and would likely lead to incremental advancement, at best. To achieve a disruptive outcome, thoughts must be gathered from myriad sources and the sources should be as diverse as possible. This notion is elaborated on by Everett Rogers in his book "Diffusion of Innovations" where he expounds on the topic of "heterophily" (Rogers, 2016). In short, the more the thought contributors vary in background, beliefs and culture, the wider the perspectives on the innovation ideas. Such engagements have the best potential for disruptive innovations.

In this context, the term "disruptive" is viewed in a positive light, because innovation offers the potential of greater value than the status quo and it changes actions and behaviors for the benefit of the audiences of the innovation. In addition to opening up the thought aperture to gain the broadest perspective, the innovator teaches others in the organization how to share knowledge in the process of coming up with new ideas in the pursuit of the next innovation for the organization. Any innovation resulting from the collaboration with a diverse team of thought contributors is likely to appeal to a broad range of customers in the market. Along with an open mind, innovators must crave any criticism related to the idea they wish to turn into an innovation. Any criticism offered by people in relevant roles represents a clear view of obstacles the innovator must overcome to gain the confidence and support of those offering the criticism. These people do not possess the vision of the innovator and are not yet convinced that the idea offers the value espoused by the innovator. These criticisms are called "fears" and if the innovator takes them at face value, the path to overcoming the fears is made clear. In some literature, fears are referred to as "barriers" to innovation because they tend to stifle innovative thought and action. Innovators should never argue with people about their fears. Innovators should instead take the people by the [figurative] hand and help them to overcome their fears and to demonstrate the value of the idea through experimentation. More discussion on this topic is covered later.

In the context of an innovation pursuit, ideas put forth by contributors or innovators may encounter resistance from people serving in various roles within the organization. The basis of the resistance is categorized as a "fear". Fears may be recognized by the language used to express resistance to ideas. For instance:

✦ "We tried this idea 5 years ago, so we know it will not work today"
✦ "There is no way we can do better than the system in place now"
✦ "The proposed idea will not fit our business model"
✦ "This idea is too complicated for our workforce"

Fears represent risk to the people who think the idea will cause more issues than benefits. In a study published by the Defense Innovation Board (DIB) – Lowering the Barriers to Innovation, the statement captures the relevance of overcoming barriers: "Our ability to ensure enduring technological superiority hinges on how fast we can remove the barriers internal to the Department that hamper innovation adoption" (DIB, 2024)

Innovators have a strong creative drive. They are able to connect seemingly unrelated ideas, think outside the box, and generate novel solutions to problems, sometimes using readily available materials and technologies. They employ divergent thinking skills to explore multiple possibilities and convergent thinking skills to evaluate and refine ideas (DeGraff, 2020). In other words, innovators examine the status quo offerings, examine their shortcomings and propose new and better ways to offer value to existing and future customers and stakeholders. Please note that just because a product currently exists, there are numerous ways to reimagine the look, feel, color, weight, size, shape and general utility of the product. To this point, the U.S. Patent and Trademark Office, since its establishment, has granted nearly 5000 patents with the term "mouse trap" in their respective titles. No wonder the quote "there is always a better way to build a mouse trap" is commonly uttered in conversations when discussing innovations. Creativity is essential when attempting to make distinctions between the organization's offering and something that may exist in the market that was produced by a competitor.

An innovative mindset involves a willingness to take calculated risks. Innovators understand that failure is a natural part of the learning process and are not afraid to experiment and try new things. They have a bias towards action and are willing to step out of their respective comfort zones to pursue new opportunities. This mental disposition of the innovator does not imply a sense of recklessness, but more of a desire to step outside of the traditional path to pursue a potential innovation that benefits the organization (Dyer, 2019). Risk-taking is beneficial because there is learning and a potential bottom-line gain to be realized. There is, however, there is the possibility that the organization stands to lose more than it gains in the innovation pursuit, too. This possibility is tempered by setting in place an agreed upon percentage of time, effort and resources to pursue the idea. In such cases, if the innovation cannot be realized, any losses are minimized in the pursuit.

Innovators are resilient in the face of challenges and setbacks. They view failure as a learning opportunity and are able to bounce back quickly (Mejia, 2022). They have a growth mindset, believing that their abilities can be developed through dedication and hard work. In the case of a setback, innovators must put distance between themselves and the innovation they are pursuing. For instance, if innovators get too involved in the fate of the innovation pursuit, if it fails, they may take the failure personally. That position can lead to a negative hit on the innovator's level of confidence, because a failure in the pursuit may result in them feeling personally responsible for the fate of the pursuit. Ideally, the innovators must be shielded from the fate of the innovation pursuit. The innovators are the champions that make certain the idea or concept gets the best opportunity to become the envisioned innovation, but if it fails to reach expectations, it simply means that the conditions were not favorable to reach the desired outcome. So, distance must be put between the innovators and the ideas they champion in any potentially negative outcome from the innovation pursuit.

An innovative mindset recognizes the power of collaboration. Innovators actively seek out opportunities to work with others, knowing that diverse perspectives and skill sets can lead to better ideas and outcomes. They are skilled at building relationships, communicating effectively, and fostering a sense of shared purpose. Innovators realize that even though they represent the driving force in the innovation pursuit, they do not possess all the required knowledge, skills and access to the relevant networks of people who can help move the innovation idea toward the goal of becoming an innovation (Mollman, 2022). To that end, innovators must seek help to perform various roles during the pursuit.

Additionally, innovators cannot afford to get bogged down in the low-level activities of proving the value of the innovation and lowering the innovation's risk profile to help ensure the capture of required resources to keep the pursuit active and avoid fast failure exit condition. Instead, they must shepherd the idea through the innovation process to ensure the risk reduction (i.e., de-risking) and value exposure occurs along the path.

Innovators are deeply attuned to the needs and desires of their customers or end-users. Innovators must empathize with their target audience, seek to understand their pain points and aspirations, and use these insights to drive meaningful innovations that create value (Hughes, Chapnick, Block and Saptak, 2021).. Whether imagining the success of the innovation for an entire market or a single customer, the innovator must keep an open mind and think outside the box. They must also understand when to apply the necessary constraints, too. If customers are inter-ested in acquiring products derived from the innovation but the size of the product has to fit within a defined physical space and with a specific shape, these are considerations that directly affect the manufacturability of the product. Additionally, customers may not exist only in the targeted external market. Some cus-tomers may be internal to the organization and deserve just as much consideration as the external customers when crafting and de-risking ideas that form the basis of the innovation. The basic idea is the same for the innovators. They must understand the customer goals and the constraints and make those prime con-siderations during the relevant phases of the innovation process so that an understanding of the resulting innovation is practical and cost effective for the organization and the customer.

An innovative mindset is highly adaptable. Innovators are comfortable with change and uncertainty. They are able to pivot quickly when faced with new information or changing circumstances, and they are always looking for ways to improve and evolve. A common characteristic of innovative organizations that continue to flourish as the time changes are those that are able to foresee and adapt to change (Sellar, and Anthonypillai, 2023). In short, the organization and its workforce should not fall in love with the status quo. They must adjust and move forward by adapting to the changes in the market, forced by their competitors or they cause the market to change and force their competitors to adapt. Innovators in this environment must consider the fluidity of the environment as they propose new ideas for innovation, or they modify (in progress) innovation pursuits such that they can survive and thrive in the new marketplace.

Innovators need to develop a long-term perspective. They anticipate and monitor emerging trends, envision new possibilities, and work towards creating a better future. They are not constrained by the status quo and are willing to disrupt existing systems and paradigms to drive progress (Marchand, 2022). Innovators are part visionary and part systems engineers. This simply means that they have ideas about the innovation, how it might be used, the potential value it brings to the forefront and the practicality of delivering it to the target audience at scale. They also have to think about the current technologies and any derived technologies emerging from the research environment that may be utilized in delivering a future innovation for the organization. While an innovation might be represented as a simple concept, innovators must place it in a larger context to ensure it has long-term future value, it has minimal risks, it is practical to deliver, and it provides the functionality and aesthetics to the customer at a reasonable cost.

An innovator's mindset is fueled by a strong sense of passion and purpose. Innovators are intrinsically motivated by the desire to make a positive impact, solve meaningful problems, and create value for others (Marchand, 2022). They are driven by a deep sense of commitment to their work and are willing to persevere through challenges to achieve their goals. Cultivating these characteristics and fostering an environment that supports and rewards innovative thinking can unlock the full potential of their human capital and drive sustainable growth. Every innovation is the product of an initial idea, the passion of the person who wants to see it succeed and a process that identifies and resolves risks to increase its odds of becoming a big hit. The innovation is a manifestation of numerous conversations, arguments and agreements occurring around ideas that are offered and pursued.

Breaking away from the status quo, putting forth an idea, taking on the responsibilities and challenges of pursuing something new is exciting and rewarding, but innovation does not occur in isolation. The process of creating the desired change through an innovation process requires transforming the mindset of people in the crowd to play an active role in taking their ideas from conception through fruition. This social engagement is necessary to create innovators that shepherd ideas from inception to realization. Such innovators play a critical role in any innovation process, and they are essential to an organization that is transforming itself from the status quo to position itself on a more innovative footing.

CHAPTER 3

Identifying and Overcoming Mental Barriers to Innovation

"The greatest danger in times of turbulence is not the turbulence; it is to act with yesterday's logic."

—Peter Drucker

Identifying and overcoming mental barriers to innovation is crucial for fostering a culture of creativity and continuous improvement. There are, however, strategies to help individuals and organizations break through barriers to innovation. In this chapter, these strategies are explored to provide the innovator with helpful perspectives to recognize and overcome barriers to innovation. The first step, for instance, is to recognize and acknowledge the existence of mental barriers. Organizational leaders must encourage open discussions about the common mental blocks that hinder innovation, such as fear of failure, resistance to change, or fixed mindsets. Bringing these barriers to the surface allows innovators to begin developing approaches to overcome them (DIB, 2024). Included in the previous statement is one of the biggest mental barriers to innovation, the fear of failure. This topic will receive additional attention in a later section. To overcome this fear, organizations should reframe failure as a learning opportunity. Experimentation and risk-taking must be encouraged and celebrated. In such processes, innovators are likely to experience numerous failures as they proceed along the path or potential innovation success. The lessons learned from such failures should be valued as key knowledge and shared to enhance corporate growth. This approach also helps to create an environment where people feel comfortable sharing their ideas and experiences without fear of judgment or retribution. "When the perception of interpersonal safety is high, individuals are likely to speak up, disagree, or provide critique in group settings without fear of personal retribution" (Barhydt, 2023).

To promote more curiosity within the workforce, a permission structure should be considered to encourage the asking of questions, exploring new ideas, and challenging assumptions. Although curiosity was highlighted in the previous chapter as a characteristic of an innovative mindset, it also plays a crucial role in helping to overcome barriers to innovation (Thackston, 2014). Employees should be encouraged to seek out diverse perspectives, attend conferences or workshops, and engage in continuous learning. Organizations should place a premium on providing resources and opportunities for employees to pursue their interests and expand their knowledge. Such practices may lead to more divergent thinking. Mental barriers often arise from a narrow focus or a tendency to rely on tried-and-true solutions. To break through these barriers, leaders are encouraged to promote divergent thinking techniques such as brainstorming, mind mapping, or lateral thinking. Employees should be encouraged to generate multiple ideas, defer judgment, and build upon each other's suggestions. Such techniques are popular to create the largest set of ideas because opportunities to deep dive on any topic during the process are not allowed.

Assumptions and biases can limit innovative thinking. To get the best possible results, all opinions of ideas should be examined from positive and negative perspectives, respectively. Rather than insisting that positive comments are welcomed, employees should routinely question the assumptions and look at problems from different angles. Use techniques like "assumption reversal" to uncover underlying beliefs and explore alternative perspectives (Isaksen, 2010). On the other hand, however, mental barriers arise from a perception of too much freedom or a lack of direction. Counterintuitively, embracing constraints can actually stimulate creativity. Set clear boundaries, timelines, or resource limitations to force employees to think creatively within those parameters. Constraints can often lead to more focused and innovative solutions. Employees must be equipped with the skills and tools they need to overcome mental barriers. Organizations should offer and encourage their people to take advantage of training on creative problem-solving or mindfulness practices is also an approach that should be considered to build knowledge and skill within the workforce. In addition, organizations may benefit their employees by providing access to coaches, mentors, or innovation facilitators who can guide them through the innovation process and help them navigate mental roadblocks is also an important consideration.

Diversity, as mentioned earlier, must play a significant role within innovation. Diverse teams bring a range of perspectives, experiences, and thinking styles to the table. Encouraging cross-functional collaboration and building teams with a mix of backgrounds, ages, and expertise goes a long way to helping people to feel that they are valued, and their respective contributions are meaningful. Exposure to different viewpoints can help break through mental barriers and spark new ideas (Teichert, 2023). To keep all levels of the organization involved, the organization should engage in celebrations that showcase innovative ideas, projects, and successes. Share stories of how employees overcame mental barriers and turned ideas into reality. Making innovation visible and highlighting it as a corporate value can reinforce a culture that embraces diversity, creativity and risk-taking.

Leaders play a crucial role in shaping the culture and mindset of their organizations. Organizations must insist that their leaders model innovative behaviors, share their own experiences with overcoming mental barriers, and create an environment that supports and rewards innovative thinking. Remember, overcoming mental barriers to innovation is an ongoing process that requires patience, persistence, and a commitment to continuous learning and growth. Implementing the named strategies and fostering a culture that values creativity and experimentation is beneficial in realizing meaningful innovation.

CHAPTER 4

Fostering a Growth Mindset

*"The mind is not a vessel to be filled
but a fire to be kindled."*

—Plutarch

Fostering a growth mindset throughout an organization is essential for creating a culture of continuous learning, improvement, and innovation. A growth mindset, as coined by psychologist Carol Dweck, is the belief that abilities and intelligence can be developed through dedication and hard work (Dweck, 2006). There are recommended approaches to cultivate a growth mindset at both the individual and organizational levels. One such way, for instance, is to provide training and resources to help employees understand the concept of growth mindset and its benefits. Communicate the importance of a growth mindset through various channels, such as workshops, newsletters, or internal campaigns. Encourage leaders to openly discuss their own learning journeys and share stories of growth and development.

Leaders can help create a culture that values continuous learning and provides opportunities for employees to develop new skills and knowledge (Fonseca, Silva, Silva & Pereira, 2019). They can offer training programs, workshops, and e-learning resources that cater to different learning styles and needs. Employees should be encouraged to set learning goals, attend conferences, and seek out mentorship or coaching opportunities. Another innovative approach to encourage learning and development is to form partner relationships with book publishers and training organizations to offer deeply discounted training opportunities for their employees.

More forward-leaning organizations have instituted specialized educational opportunities in partnership with local universities. Some of these programs have spurred new degree offerings by the universities and they enhance the educational credentials of the organization's employees by advancing their degree holdings. The offering of educational opportunities to the employees attracts talent to the organization and builds on the knowledge and expertise of the organization.

Such programs serve to continually upgrade the knowledge and skills of the collective workforce. These intellectual gains directly benefit the employee and the organization. When an organization invests in the growth of the people it employs, the employees feel valued and will perform more work and do it at a higher level.

People are generally conditioned to view failure as a negative outcome, but that viewpoint should be recast as learning opportunities instead. The business must continuously promote a culture that views challenges and failures as opportunities for growth and learning. In order for employees to embrace challenges, they have to take calculated risks and learn from their mistakes. At the same time, however, they need to be given the latitude to think and work outside the box. If the organization begins to celebrate the lessons learned from failures and share success stories of individuals who have overcome obstacles and achieved growth, they may be inclined to take more chances.

The organization's view and behavior concerning the topic of failure is crucial in determining the success of establishing and building a culture of innovation. The framework and processes resulting from the organizational view goes a long way in the minds of the members of the workforce and that determines the corporate level of risk tolerance. Keep in mind that if an organization is unwilling to take risks, the long-term viability of the organization may be in jeopardy. While there is no certainty in the previous statement, there are scores of organizations that barreled into obsolescence because of their unwillingness or inability to overcome their averseness to risk-taking and thinking beyond the proverbial box.

In professional environments, there are words that are showstoppers when it comes to an organization's ability to portray success. When the goals of the organization's strategy are satisfied, contributors are rewarded and given positive recognition. As a result, their respective urban legend as potential "unicorns" is increased. When outcomes do not achieve their intended goals, however, the attempt is cast as a failure and a stigma is attached to anyone who played a role in the resulting outcome. So, is it possible to succeed at meeting all the goals? Does the expectation of success make people less adventurous to try new ideas? The way an organization behaves when outcomes are less than optimal defines the long-term viability of the organization. How are members of the organization likely to perceive risk-taking in an environment that operates with a binary (i.e., Succeed or Fail) reward philosophy? In addition, what types of behaviors are encouraged and discouraged in such environments? Since the discussion emphasizes the establishment and growth of an innovation culture, what considerations should be considered for developing the proper mindset and behaviors to benefit the organization and its members?

As mentioned, when failure occurs (by the organization's standards), the outcome may be viewed negatively and reflect poorly on the organization and its members. As an example, an organization may invest in workforce training, for instance, to improve their respective knowledge and understanding about topics important to the organization. Within the training course, people may be given challenge problems that help them to better understand and master the topic. As people engage in the problems, they are asked questions and are expected to answer them correctly. Because they are becoming familiar with the topics and mastery has not yet been achieved, they answer some of the questions incorrectly. Did they fail the course? No! The students can ask questions, re-work the problems and get additional help from the course instructor.

So, in the context of learning, doing something incorrectly is not considered a failure. It is considered a necessary part of the learning experience. What would happen if employers viewed failure as learning, instead? Would it have an impact on employees taking more risks or simply trying different approaches to get the work done? Absolutely.

Organizations must innovate to succeed. To succeed at anything, attempts must be made to try something different than the status quo (Friedman, 2012). In these attempts, discoveries are made that potentially add value to the organization's bottom line. In the attempts, however, planned outcomes are not always achieved. The attitudes about the "failed" outcomes must be treated as learning events that enrich the knowledge of the organization. After all, the success of the famed light bulb was preceded by roughly 1,000 attempts.

The trails leading to the eventual desired outcome are always paved with failures. Those failures are necessary for the organization to achieve its ultimate goals. Remember the failures are learning events that provide the necessary insights to achieve the desired outcome.

Another typical example of organizational behavior is the recognition of success. Sometimes ceremonies are held to show recognition to employees who have succeeded in some endeavor that the organization holds in high esteem. This recognition comes at the end of the work that led to the success. What about the employees who dared to step outside their respective comfort zones to help make the final outcome possible? Shouldn't they be recognized, as well? The attempts to achieve the desired outcome that were not viewed as successful expanded the knowledge base of the organization. Of course, their efforts should be rewarded.

Organizations need to establish additional categories of recognition to highlight the value that the organization places on risk-taking within the organization. This concept provides the requisite encouragement to the workforce to think and act outside of the box into which they work every day.

If the traditional stigma associated with failure is recast by the organization as a positive attribute, people may feel more emboldened and try new methods for doing their respective work. The organization must not only tolerate such behaviors but enthusiastically encourage them as well.

When employees understand that their ideas are contributing to the success of the organization and that their attempts at bettering the organization will be rewarded, they are more likely to participate in trying new ideas to innovate for the organization.

Just as the cybersecurity industry has gained notoriety in recent years, there is a heavy emphasis on innovation. Business entities in public, private and academic settings are seeking innovators to help expand their respective services, products, and influence, accordingly. These entities commonly express that they wish to establish and grow a culture of innovation in their respective organizations. If they can achieve such an outcome, it will come about when attempts made by their respective employees will be celebrated, and not discouraged. In fact, they may be rewarded for introducing new corporate learning, which ultimately helps the organization to remain viable for the long-term.

Organizations must embrace failure, account for it, solicit ideas from their employee base (and customers) to push the envelope in the pursuit of the desired innovations. Failure is a necessary component of any effort that eventually turns into a success. The attitudes toward failure must be recast as learning epochs that are required to achieve the desired end state. Casting failure in a negative light causes people to not try new ideas. If the goal of an organization is to establish and grow a culture of innovation, then failure must not simply be tolerated, but celebrated. Failure can be a catalyst to motivate people to share their ideas and make active attempts in pursuing those ideas without the fear or organizational repercussions if the desired outcome is not optimal. Organizations must change their perspectives on failure and the innovation culture will materialize and grow accordingly.

Feedback is crucial for fostering a growth mindset. Employees must be provided regular, constructive feedback that focuses on effort, progress, and learning rather than just outcomes. Feedback may be used as an opportunity to identify areas for improvement and provide guidance and support for development. Organizations must foster a culture of open, two-way feedback where employees feel comfortable seeking and providing feedback to others. In some progressive business environments, employees may be free to provide feedback to their immediate supervisors using a term called "managing up". This engagement can be effective to inform the managers of the direct and indirect implications of the direction to employees. In either case of managing up or down, feedback must be clear, unambiguous and actionable. Feedback should not be given just for the sake of satisfying an organizational imperative to entertain such conversations as a regular part of business operations.

Traditionally, organizations focus on bottom-line outcomes as the indication of success and pay little attention to the effort expended to reach the outcome. Additionally, heroic efforts that produce tremendous learnings seem to go unnoticed when the desired outcome is not reached.

Organizations must change their measures of success to keep their people motivated about innovation. New knowledge is created during every innovative pursuit even if the ultimate outcome is not achieved. Innovators must be recognized for their respective efforts because the knowledge gained through the pursuit can be leveraged in subsequent pursuits that lead to the desired outcomes.

Recognize and reward employees who demonstrate a growth mindset, whether through their willingness to take on new challenges, their openness to feedback, or their commitment to learning and development. Celebrate milestones and achievements that showcase growth and improvement. Consider incorporating growth mindset competencies into performance evaluations and promotion criteria.

Another essential emphasis area is the fostering of a culture that encourages experimentation, iteration, and continuous improvement. Provide opportunities for employees to test new ideas, prototype solutions, and refine their approaches based on feedback and learning (Puspitasari, Atmojo and Daryanto, 2024). Emphasize the value of the learning process rather than just the end result.

The organization should continuously encourage collaboration and knowledge sharing across teams and departments. Another helpful step is to create opportunities for employees to work on cross-functional projects, participate in peer learning groups, or engage in knowledge-sharing sessions. Foster a culture where employees feel comfortable asking for help, sharing their expertise, and learning from one another (Mollman, 2022).

Leaders play a crucial role in shaping the mindset and culture of their organizations. Leaders should model growth mindset behaviors, such as admitting when they don't know something, seeking feedback, and showing a willingness to learn and improve. Leaders should also create environments where people feel comfortable taking risks and expressing ideas without fear of judgment or retribution. Leaders must also ensure that organizational systems and processes support and reinforce a growth mindset culture. This may involve adjusting performance management systems to focus on learning and development, creating innovation labs or incubators to support experimentation, or providing resources and budgets for employee development initiatives.

Regularly measure and assess the organization's progress in fostering a growth mindset culture. Accurate assessment methods have historically been inaccurate. "They frequently disregard the perspectives and needs of practitioners who are actively participating in the innovation process. This misalignment results in a noticeable gap between those actively "doing" innovation and those tasked with measuring it" (Misra, 2024). Use employee surveys, focus groups, or other assessment tools to gauge mindset shifts and identify areas for improvement. Celebrate successes and share stories of growth and development to reinforce the importance of a growth mindset. Implementing these approaches and consistently reinforcing the value of a growth mindset reinforces cultural values of learning, innovation, and continuous.

PART II

Building an Innovation Culture

CHAPTER 5

The Elements of an Innovation Culture

"Culture eats strategy for breakfast."

—Unknown

A n innovation culture is a set of shared values, beliefs, and behaviors that support and encourage the continuous pursuit of new ideas, creativity, and improvement within an organization. Building a strong innovation culture is essential for organizations to stay competitive, adapt to change, and drive long-term success. There are key elements of an innovation culture that require further elaboration.

Leaders play a crucial role in shaping and driving an innovation culture. They are responsible for articulating a clear, compelling vision for innovation and communicating its importance to the organization. If leaders desire to create and grow a culture of innovation, they have to model innovative behaviors, encourage risk-taking, and provide the necessary resources and support for innovation initiatives. The visionary leader must set a vision that is ambitious yet attainable. They must plan to realize the vision enabled through the fostering of a culture of innovation and adaptability, encouraging experimentation, and embracing change as necessary for organizational success and continual growth. Leaders have to plot a new path forward by challenging the status quo to drive innovation across all aspects of the organization. One practice developed by the Pfizer corporation encourages leaders to see the good in offered ideas, visualize the potential opportunities and benefits if the innovation is realized, consider some of the challenges to a successful outcome and inject new thinking for raised issues (Horth and Mitchell, 2024). Leadership direction has to be clear, foster trust and accountability, and nurturing talent development to ensure that everyone can contribute their best. Another thing that strong leaders do is lead by example, and they embody the values and behaviors that are core to the organization's culture. In all facets of leadership, they demonstrate integrity, resilience, and a commitment to excellence in every facet of the role. While others focus on issues that are near-term, leaders prioritize long-term sustainability over short-term gains, considering the impact of our decisions on stakeholders, the environment, and society as a whole. Leaders inspire confidence and trust in the workforce and the organization's stakeholders by demonstrating competence, vision, and integrity.

An innovation culture thrives on providing a safe space in which people can express ideas, take risks, and make mistakes without fear of judgment, ridicule, or retribution. Leaders must create an environment of trust, openness, and respect, where employees feel comfortable sharing their thoughts, challenging the status quo, and experimenting with new approaches (Barhydt,

2023). In psychologically safe environments, team members feel accepted, respected, and valued for their contributions, fostering an atmosphere of trust, open communication, and collaboration.

In an innovative organization, psychological safety plays a crucial role. One such role is promoting openness and idea sharing. This openness creates a fertile ground for brainstorming, creativity, and the exploration of new possibilities, leading to the generation of innovative solutions to complex problems. Innovation involves taking risks and experimenting with new approaches. Employees need to feel comfortable taking calculated risks without the fear of ridicule or punishment if things don't go as planned. The freedom to experiment fosters a culture of innovation where new ideas can be tested, refined, and implemented without the fear of failure. When people encouraged to take risks in pursuing their respective ideas without career threatening consequences, the business entity's thought space expands. When employees feel psychologically safe, they are more likely to seek feedback, collaborate, ask questions, and admit mistakes, knowing that they won't be judged or criticized harshly (Kahn, 1990). This creates an environment of continuous learning and improvement, where individuals are encouraged to reflect on their experiences, learn from failures, and adapt their approach in pursuit of innovation. Such an environment attracts and retains talent.

Entities that prioritize psychological safety tend to attract top talent who seek environments where they can thrive, contribute meaningfully, and grow professionally. Moreover, employees are more likely to stay with organizations that prioritize their well-being and provide a supportive and inclusive culture, reducing turnover and retaining valuable knowledge and expertise within the organization. Organizations that create an environment where they can realize the full potential of their teams and drive sustainable innovation and success.

Innovators travel a lonely road as visionaries that see things that their leaders, peers and subordinates may not support. If an idea is to reach the goal of becoming an adopted innovation, the innovator must be focused on the tasks ahead, show resilience and maintain the belief that the pursuit is worthwhile. Innovators may feel the sting of ridicule and scorn from people who do not share the same vision and could become discouraged. If this type of environment is allowed to persist, innovators will not feel compelled or encouraged to pursue their respective visions.

One way to help foster a psychologically safe environment is to actively demonstrate support for the innovators validating them and their pursuit and offering words of encouragement to keep them engaged. The act of rallying around innovators to show them that they have a great team and organizational support can mean the difference in them staying on course in pursuing their ideas or bolting for the exit door. When innovators become bewildered, for whatever reason, they require validation and encouragement. This idea led to the novel approach of writing them Letters Of Validation and Encouragement (a.k.a. LOVE letters). Innovation sounds like a glamourous term but the act of innovating is a tough and arduous slog. The process of transforming incomplete ideas into practical innovative solutions is taxing and innovators may get discouraged along the way. Some innovators need validation that they are pursuing a legitimate line of pursuit. Others may require encouragement to keep pressing forward in hopes of realizing the desired outcome. The following is a contrived love letter exemplar that demonstrates the points made to refocus the innovator and get them back into the innovation pursuit:

Dear Innovator,

I'm reaching out to offer my support and admiration for your innovative manufacturing solution. Your dedication in the face of skepticism is truly commendable. I've been following your progress, and the viability you've demonstrated is impressive. Remember, many groundbreaking innovations were initially met with disbelief. Your situation is no different, and it doesn't diminish the value of your contribution. While it's natural to feel discouraged when colleagues don't immediately see the potential, view this as an opportunity to refine your presentation and strengthen your arguments. Your ability to see solutions where others see only problems is a rare gift. The manufacturing issue you're addressing is pressing, and your approach could be the key to solving it. Don't let the current lack of faith dim your belief in what you've created. The potential impact of your innovation extends far beyond proving others wrong – it has the power to transform our processes and influence the entire industry.

As you navigate these challenges, know that you're not alone. I'm here if you need to discuss strategies or simply need a reminder of how valuable your work is. Your resilience is a testament to your character and the strength of your innovation. Keep pushing forward, refining, and believing in your vision. The path of innovation is rarely smooth, but it's innovators like you who change the world. I have full faith in you and your idea. The manufacturing world needs your innovation, even if not everyone sees it yet. Stay the course. Your perseverance will pay off.

Sincerely,

John Doe,
Innovation Coach

In order to reassure and reinforce the innovators to forge ahead in their pursuits, the innovation coaches can cheer on and rally behind the innovators to keep them interested and motivated to move forward. One way to keep the energy levels of the innovators up and their attention on the innovation is to write them letters to validate them and their innovation pursuits. In addition, the letters provide sources of encouragement to let the innovators know that they are not alone in their pursuit of that major disruptive innovation.

Innovators must know that they can walk away from the process at any time. Sometimes, innovators lose faith that their ideas will be transformed into the next big innovation. When this happens, they require support. When adequate support is not given, some of them may bolt for the exit door. In many cases, positive words from trusted parties may be the only thing that motivates innovators to stay in the game and move forward in the process. The knowledge that all innovation participants share as an innovation culture norm is the ability to disengage and walk away from the pursuit at any time. This norm may be instituted, for example, to lower the level of pressure the innovator may feel as it relates to their respective innovation pursuit. Pressure may also be felt from the desire to succeed personally or for the organization.

Why in the world would innovators change their minds about ideas they initially piqued their interests.? Remember that innovators are typically ahead of everyone else's time. Other people who do not see or buy into the innovator's vision may offer discouraging thoughts and convince the innovator to pursue "more reasonable" ideas. Innovators may also be told that their idea has been tried before and failed. They also may be told their idea is impractical and nobody is likely to support it. Such feedback to the innovator can easily discourage and demotivate them to continue. This bombardment of negativity requires continual countering through validation, inspiration, and motivation to continue.

While innovating is not as glamorous as it may be depicted on television (e.g. Shark Tank), it can produce great rewards if innovators stay focused and limit negative distractions. Innovators expect to get some amount of discouraging feedback along the path, but too much negativity may directly affect the innovator's motivation to keep going. Love letters provide a means of validating the innovators chosen pursuit and encourages them to keep up the momentum while muffling the voices of doubt. As a tool, love letters can make the difference between a successful innovation or an innovator full of despair and an abandoned pursuit. IIRs use love letters as a subtle way to keep the innovator focused and motivated to stay engaged and not run away from the process.

Diversity of thought, background, and experience is a key driver of innovation. An innovation culture values and leverages the diverse perspectives and skills of its employees. It actively seeks out and includes underrepresented voices, fosters inclusive collaboration, and encourages cross-functional teamwork to spark new ideas and solutions.

Diversity and inclusion play a crucial role in fostering an innovation culture within an organization. It brings together individuals with a range of backgrounds, experiences, and perspectives (Forbes, 2011). When people with diverse viewpoints collaborate, they bring unique insights to problem-solving and decision-making processes. This diversity of thought sparks creativity and innovation by challenging conventional thinking and encouraging the exploration of alternative solutions (Kuratko, 2018).

A diverse workforce better reflects the customers and markets served by the organization. By embracing diversity, organizations gain access to valuable insights into the needs, preferences, and behaviors of diverse customer segments. This understanding enables them to develop products, services, and marketing strategies that resonate with a broader range of customers, driving innovation and competitive advantage. Understanding and embracing the differences in people, fostering inclusion, and creating environments where everyone feels valued and empowered to contribute is essential to drive creativity and reinforce the corporate innovation culture (Forbes, 2011).

An innovation culture is deeply focused on understanding and meeting the needs of customers or end-users. It encourages employees to empathize with customers, gather insights through research and feedback, and use these insights to drive meaningful innovations that create value. Customer-centricity helps ensure that innovations are relevant, desirable, and sustainable. Customer centricity is a business approach that puts the customer at the center of everything the company does. It's not just about providing good customer service, but about understanding your customers deeply and using that understanding to shape all your decisions.

When an organization is customer is placed at the center of innovation efforts, there is a deep concentration on the customer and its wants, needs and motivations. The organization aspires to create positive experiences for customers at every touch-point, from marketing and sales to product development and customer support. Employees are equipped with the knowledge and resources they need to make decisions that are in the best interest of the customer. Entities that are truly customer-centric are more likely to retain customer loyalty, command premium prices, attract and retain top talent and be more innovative and responsive to changing Customer centricity, therefore, is a way of doing business that puts the customer first and builds strong, lasting relationships.

An innovation culture encourages experimentation, iteration, and calculated risk-taking. It provides opportunities for employees to test new ideas, prototype solutions, and learn from failures. It celebrates the learning process and recognizes that not all experiments will succeed. This approach helps organizations quickly validate ideas, refine solutions, and adapt to changing circumstances. An innovation culture values continuous learning and growth at both the individual and organizational levels. It provides opportunities for employees to develop new skills, acquire knowledge, and stay up to date with industry trends and technologies. It encourages knowledge sharing, mentorship, and peer learning to foster a culture of continuous improvement.

Innovation often requires the ability to pivot quickly in response to new information, changing market conditions, or emerging opportunities (Kuratko, 2018). An innovation culture promotes agility and adaptability, encouraging employees to embrace change, make data-driven decisions, and adjust their approaches as needed (Catmull, 2014). It values flexibility and responsiveness over rigid processes and hierarchies.

Innovation rarely happens in isolation. An innovation culture fosters collaboration and teamwork, recognizing that the best ideas often emerge from the collective intelligence of diverse groups. It encourages cross-functional collaboration, breaks down silos, and provides tools and spaces for employees to work together effectively.

While members of the workforce may benefit from granted time to explore their ideas, they will need the necessary support to do so. Organizations quickly learn that hiring a whole new set of people to drive the innovation activities is not practical. While specialized talent in innovation methodologies may be necessary, the other personnel to be involved in the activities can be existing employees. In fact, anyone in the organization can participate in the innovation activity through voluntary action. Leaders, managers and employees must have a meeting of the minds to craft a system whereby the ground rules are established and honored for all participants in the innovation activities.

An innovation culture recognizes and rewards innovative behaviors, ideas, and successes. It celebrates the contributions of individuals and teams who drive innovation, whether through formal recognition programs, bonuses, or other incentives. It also recognizes the value of learning from failures and encourages employees to share their experiences and insights.

An innovation culture aligns its efforts with the organization's overall purpose, mission, and values. It ensures that innovations not only drive business success but also contribute to the greater good of society and the environment. This alignment helps employees find meaning and purpose in their work and fosters a sense of shared responsibility for driving positive change.

Nurturing these key elements builds a strong, sustainable innovation culture that engages employees, creates and maintains customer loyalty, and increases organizational viability over the long-term (Sloan, 2007).

CHAPTER 6

Leadership's Role in Shaping and Nurturing an Innovation Culture

"Logic will get you from A to B.
Imagination will take you everywhere."

—Albert Einstein

Leadership plays a critical role in shaping and nurturing an organization's innovation culture. Leaders at all levels, from top executives to front-line managers, have the power to create an environment that either supports or stifles innovation (Horth, 2024). Leaders, in fact, set the vision and strategy of the organization. They also play a huge role in establishing and maintaining the organizational culture. The organizational performance and its corporate behavior are reflections of the people who sit atop the organization. Such influence is essential when transforming traditional organizations into innovation-driven organizations. Leaders must articulate a clear, compelling vision for innovation that aligns with the organization's overall purpose and goals. They should communicate the importance of innovation to the organization's success and define the strategic priorities and focus areas for innovation efforts. This vision should inspire and engage employees, customers, and stakeholders.

Leaders must demonstrate to the workforce the behaviors to indicate a shift in the organizational footing. A common refrain in the leadership domain is to "lead by example". So, how do leaders lead by example? Leaders must begin by modeling the behaviors and mindsets they wish to see in their employees. They should demonstrate curiosity, openness to new ideas, willingness to take risks, and resilience in the face of setbacks (Horth, 2024). Leaders who embody these characteristics can inspire and empower others to embrace innovation in their own work. As evidence of the mind shift, a tangible difference is the language used by leaders to communicate. Instead of the authoritarian approach of issuing directives that the workforce must follow, leaders can instead solicit ideas from the workforce and indicate that they are important irreplaceable parts of the organization. Leaders may also express that thinking outside of the box is encouraged and expected to help the organization achieve its goals. With such declarations and acts, the workforce is likely to begin reflecting back on these behaviors and actions as they move forward in time.

"Trust is the first law of innovation" (Coffman, 2006). Trust is a big factor as to whether an organization can make the shift to become more innovative. The workforce must trust that the words spoken by the leaders are authentic and there is action that makes the words more concrete. If, for instance, an employee tries to modify an existing process to make it more efficient and it fails to meet expectations, will that employee experience negative consequences, or will their efforts be celebrated as a learning experience for the organization? They should consider encouraging open communication, to help foster a culture of trust and respect (Coffman, 2006). Leaders should also be willing to acknowledge their own vulnerabilities and mistakes, showing that it's okay to be imperfect and that learning is a continuous process.

An innovation-driven organization must be equipped to work differently than a traditional organization. Working differently means the processes and tooling must be put into place to empower and enable employees to explore ideas in ways that go beyond the existing capabilities. Leaders must empower employees to take ownership of innovation and commit to providing them with the resources, tools, and support they need to succeed. This may involve providing training and development opportunities, allocating time and budgets for innovation projects, or creating dedicated innovation teams or roles. Leaders should also remove barriers to innovation, such as bureaucratic processes or risk-averse policies. Once the tooling is in place and the barriers removed, workers can exercise their creativity in new and exciting ways. Encouraging experimentation and risk-taking are innovation concepts that must be embraced by the organization (Thomke, 2001). Leaders must encourage experimentation and calculated risk-taking, recognizing that not all ideas will succeed but that the learning process is valuable. They should provide opportunities for employees to test and validate ideas, gather feedback, and iterate on solutions. Leaders should also celebrate the lessons learned from failures and share success stories to reinforce the value of experimentation.

Leaders must convey that the organization as a whole must grow, and this requires employees working together and sharing ideas on a routine basis. Leaders must therefore encourage collaboration and cross-functional teamwork as a general way of doing internal business (Gunaratne, 2001). Leaders must work to gray the lines between silos and encourage collaboration across teams, departments, and functions. They should create opportunities for diverse groups to work together on innovation projects, share knowledge and insights, and build on each other's ideas. Leaders should also foster external partnerships and collaborations to bring in fresh perspectives and expertise. Additionally, leaders must ensure that organizational systems and processes support and reinforce the innovation culture. This may involve adjusting performance management systems to reward innovative behaviors and outcomes, creating innovation metrics and dashboards, or establishing governance structures for innovation initiatives. Leaders should also ensure that innovation efforts are integrated into the organization's overall strategy and operations.

To avoid the idea that the innovation push is a "one and done" proposition, leaders must consistently communicate the value and impact of innovation to employees, customers, and stakeholders. They should celebrate innovation successes, share stories of how innovations have created value, and recognize the contributions of individuals and teams. This helps to reinforce the importance of innovation and build momentum for future efforts. The establishment of an innovation newsletter or internal organizational websites that discuss innovation activities and how they are advancing the goals of the organization are excellent ways to reinforce that the embracing of innovation is making the organization more competitive, and the workforce is playing a pivotal role (Gunaratne, 2001).

Innovation requires all employees in the workforce to continuously learn and adapt to changes in the market and enabling technologies. Leaders must embrace a mindset of continuous learning and adaptation, recognizing that innovation is an ongoing journey rather than a one-time event. They should seek out new knowledge and insights, stay attuned to market and technology trends, and be willing to pivot and adjust strategies as needed. Leaders should also encourage employees to embrace learning and growth, providing opportunities for skill development and knowledge sharing. Leaders who fulfill these responsibilities create environments that nurture and sustain innovation, engaging employees, delighting customers, and driving long-term success. Building an innovation culture requires consistent effort, commitment, and leadership at all levels of the organization.

CHAPTER 7

Encouraging Experimentation

"I have not failed. I've just found 1,000 ways that won't work."

—Thomas A. Edison

I n a traditional hierarchical organization where the workforce is accustomed to working within a rigid framework, encouraging experimentation can be particularly challenging. However, there are strategies leaders can employ to gradually shift the culture and enable more innovative ways of working.

Creating spaces for experimentation is an essential show of good faith from leaders to the workforce. Leaders can create dedicated spaces, programs, or initiatives that provide a safe environment for employees to experiment with new ideas and approaches. These could be physical innovation labs or even virtual spaces where employees can collaborate and test ideas.

Leaders who provide a clear structure and guidelines for these initiatives help employees feel more comfortable stepping outside their usual roles and routines.

Keep in mind that innovation may require means that extend beyond anything the organization has used or tried in the past to achieve its goals. To the organizational leadership, this unfamiliar mental terrain implies risk. Experimentation offers a means of de-risking proposed innovations before the organizational leadership commits to investing its capital and efforts to adopt and deploy any product or service emerging from innovation processes (Thomke, 2001). This job of de-risking innovation ideas may be performed in a variety of ways such as experimentation, simulation and model scale prototype design and development. Experimentation involves addressing any expressed or perceived organizational fears about the innovation idea in a low-cost approach that helps organizational leadership better understand the risks and how to lower them to get to the point of supporting and enabling the innovation.

Fears are the reason that people and organizations opt to not pursue ideas. A fear is a doubtful thought that a person or organization uses to prohibit further investment of energy and time because they believe the result will be failure (DIB, 2024). More precisely, a fear represents a barrier to innovation success. Fears may be tested for validity through experimentation or via prototype construction and testing. As an innovator, the goal is to collect all the fears about an idea, organize them into prioritized groups of no more than three major fear categories. Then, craft experiments to test the fears to see if they have validity. A single experiment for each fear category is defined and implements a binary test yielding an outcome of pass or fail. If the test passes, the fear is not valid, otherwise the test fails, and the fear is valid.

Structuring an innovation system that relies on experimentation to address identified fears, whether rational or irrational, may be systematically tested to determine if a proposed idea is worthy of being pursued as a potential innovation. The tests are commonly referred to as fast fail gates, because they determine the pursuit value before further time and energy are expended to pursue the proposed idea. To proceed further with the idea, all fast fail gates must pass.

Physical experimentation spaces have some advantages. Members of the workforce, for instance, can see a manifestation of the organization's commitment to innovation when there is a physical place designed to encourage experimentation. Such spaces have a clear advantage to the workforce in that the facilities are accessible in the building structure in which they work.

Another feature of localized experimentation spaces is access to expertise to assist innovations in working through the various challenges of their proposed innovation pursuits. Innovators coaches are innovation masters who hang out in innovation venues and offer assistance where and when needed. Additionally, being in the presence of other fellow innovators offers comfort to those who are pursuing innovations and builds a sense of community amongst those who dared to think outside the box. What happens, however, if the organization is distributed and members of the workforce cannot easily access the facilities or the people in the experimentation spaces?

Virtual experimentation spaces may be established to offer support and enablement to employees at the main location as well as distributed locations. Access to the tooling, data and systems necessary to enable innovation pursuits can be handled successfully in such a manner. Access to the coaches and fellow innovators becomes especially challenging, however, due to time zones. Some organizations deal with this issue by providing asynchronous communications capabilities like those found in many online educational environments where students and professors exchange information by posting content that is engaged by each other in their respective time zones. While such practices are effective in relaying ideas, they are not particularly time efficient. Addressing issues of this nature may require a different means.

User experience is a critical concern for organizations because it has direct implications on the level of enthusiasm of employees who wish to innovate but their capacity to do so may diminish depending on the location at which they perform their work. Ideally, when it comes to experimentation to support an innovation pursuit, the user experience is expected to be the same, whether people are at the main organization location or deployed elsewhere around the world. Making the user experience more normal might require the use of advanced technologies to include Artificial Intelligence (AI).

While the value of experienced coaches is unquestionably high, each coach possesses domain-specific experience and can offer domain specific guidance to innovators who engage them. There is, however, a plethora of Large Language Models (LLM), however, that have been trained on a multitude of topics and may be fine-tuned to act in the capacity of numerous human coaches, where each is endowed with expertise the innovator requires to fully explore the idea under consideration. If an organization wanted to level the playing field and normalize the user experience amongst all its employees, no matter their physical location, the development and deployment of virtualized avatars to serve as AI-based coaches that can be invoked on-demand, appears to be a way of establishing a consistent means for advising and guiding innovators across the enterprise.

Organizations must also realize that many people they employ will not possess the knowledge or skills to conduct experiments on the level of a typical Science Technology Engineering and Mathematician (STEM) person. It must be noted that not all innovations are the exclusive product of STEM knowledge and experience. To remedy this situation, organizations must provide training and skill-building to enable any employee to learn how to experiment in ways that are meaningful to the organization's innovation goals. Additionally, many employees in hierarchical organizations may lack the confidence to engage in experimentation and risk-taking (Thomke, 2003). Leaders can address this by providing training and development opportunities that focus on innovation skills such as creative problem-solving, design thinking, and lean experimentation. Equipping employees with new tools and approaches helps them feel more empowered to take calculated risks and try new things.

Ideally, as the organization makes the shift from traditional to innovative posture, employees should be incentivized to move, accordingly. Leaders can assist the move by making tangible adjustments to the organizational incentive structures. They can, for instance, adjust performance metrics and incentives to illicit the desired workforce behaviors (Misra, 2024). Traditional performance metrics and incentives in hierarchical organizations often prioritize efficiency, predictability, and risk avoidance over innovation and experimentation. Leaders can start to shift this by incorporating innovation-related goals and data-driven metrics into performance evaluations, and by rewarding employees who demonstrate innovative behaviors and outcomes (Luca and Bazerman, 2024). This sends a clear signal that experimentation and risk-taking are valued and encouraged.

Workforce cultures may find it difficult to accept massive changes in a short amount of time. Leaders must start small and build momentum over time to implement the desired changes. Shifting a deeply entrenched hierarchical culture towards innovation is a gradual process that requires patience and persistence. Leaders should start with small, manageable experiments and initiatives that can demonstrate quick wins and build momentum for larger-scale change. As employees start to see the benefits of experimentation and risk-taking, they will become more open to embracing these behaviors in their own work.

Encouraging experimentation and risk-taking in a traditional hierarchical organization is not easy, but it is possible with consistent effort, leadership, and a willingness to challenge the status quo. Creating safe spaces (both physically and virtually and normalizing the user experience) provides skill-building opportunities, adjusting metrics and incentives that gradually shift the culture and enable more innovative ways of working.

CHAPTER 8

Promoting Diversity and Inclusion

"Diversity: the art of thinking independently together."

—Malcolm Forbes

Promoting diversity and inclusion is crucial for building an innovation culture where all employees feel valued, respected, and empowered to contribute their best ideas. In organizations where certain people have historically gotten the best opportunities, leaders must take proactive steps to level the playing field and create a more equitable and inclusive environment. While these topics were introduced earlier, the discussion is expanded a bit to provide the necessary insights to properly frame them for organizational success

How does an organization know where it stands on the topics of diversity and inclusion? If outsiders look at the composition of the workforce, leadership, new hires, corporate partnerships and vendors, what information gets conveyed and does their mental picture align with the intentions of the organization? There is a great way to gain the necessary insights to assess the posture of the organization. The organization can conduct a diversity and inclusion audit. The first step is to understand the current state of diversity and inclusion within the organization. Leaders should conduct a comprehensive audit that looks at demographics, hiring and promotion practices, employee engagement and satisfaction, and other key metrics. This audit should also include employee surveys and focus groups to gather qualitative insights into the experiences of different groups within the organization. While this approach can provide quantitative insights, the qualitative perspectives may be visually assessed and weigh heavier than any quantitative study results.

What happens within the workforce culture that reflects organizational values? In such cases, the organization tends to fare very well because the actions match the rhetoric. The flip side of the proverbial coin is also considered. When members of the workforce are selected for recognition, rewards, promotions, plum assignments and educational opportunities, what are the demographics of the recipients of the benefits? The opportunities visually demonstrate the organization's values. If the representation does not seem fair, it most likely is not. Leadership statements about addressing inequities within the workplace do little to assure the workforce that their contributions are valued.

Organizations must set and adhere to clear diversity and inclusion goals. Based on the findings of the audit, leaders should set clear, measurable goals for improving diversity and inclusion at all levels of the organization. These goals should be tied to the organization's overall strategy and innovation objectives and should be communicated widely to all employees. To be successful in this endeavor, the communications channels must be varied because employees get their information from numerous sources and leaders must cover a range of channels to make certain the messages are being conveyed. Leaders should also establish accountability mechanisms to ensure that progress is regularly tracked and reported in a transparent manner.

Diversity and inclusion are topics that should not be left to chance. The concepts and expected behaviors should be taught and reinforced through training to yield the desired outcomes. All employees, especially leaders and managers, should receive training on diversity, inclusion, and unconscious bias. This training should help employees at all levels to understand the value of diversity, recognize, and mitigate their own biases, and develop skills for creating inclusive environments. Training should be ongoing and reinforced through regular communications and discussions. In addition to focusing on the practices within the organization focused on improving opportunities for employees, it must be broadened, accordingly.

One critical area to highlight opportunities to broaden diversity and inclusion is in hiring and promotion practices. Sometimes tweaking existing practices is sufficient, but in other cases, revamping the entire set of practices may be required. Leaders should review and revamp hiring and promotion practices to ensure that they are fair, objective, and inclusive. This may involve implementing blind resume screening, diverse interview panels, and structured interview questions. Leaders should also set diversity targets for candidate slates and actively seek out candidates from underrepresented groups.

A construct used in many modern organizations to focus on building safe spaces and workplace equity within the workplace for underrepresented groups is the employee resource groups. Employee Resource Groups (ERGs) are voluntary, employee-led groups that bring together people with shared identities or experiences (Battye, 2024). Some organizations refer to them as "Affinity Groups". ERGs can provide a safe space for employees to connect, share challenges and successes, and advocate for change within the organization. Leaders should support and resource ERGs and use them as sounding boards for diversity and inclusion initiatives. While ERGs have become increasingly popular, there are challenges when leaders and managers restrict employees from attending ERG meetings and events during work hours. Such practices send a clear message to the workforce about the level of support the organization gives to these groups.

Organizational leaders must pay attention to the issues being put forth by people in the workforce. In the typical hierarchical organizations, the day-to-day issues rarely rise to the attention of higher-level leaders, but the symptoms cannot be ignored. If segments of the workforce constantly raise concerns about the work environment, general rudeness, exclusion from high-visibility efforts, and they're not being recognized for their contributions in favor of others, this must be addressed quickly and decisively. Such issues tend to alienate people and cause the work environment to become toxic. Conversations in such environments are characteristically brief but are laced with demeaning microaggressions. Leaders must be proactive in addressing microaggressions, bias incidents, and other forms of exclusion that can undermine psychological safety and belonging. They should provide clear channels for reporting these incidents, take swift action to investigate and address them, and communicate the outcomes to all employees (Jana and Baran, 2023). Leaders should also model inclusive language and behavior in their own interactions. Managers and workers must be provided training on proper behaviors in the workplace and the leaders must set up employee performance rating criteria to ensure adoption.

There is a clear and distinct difference in being tolerated versus being celebrated. Innovative organizations celebrate diversity and inclusion because everyone in the workforce needs to understand they are important to the organization. Leaders should actively celebrate the diversity of their employees and the value that different perspectives bring to the organization. This could involve highlighting employee stories and achievements, hosting cultural events and celebrations, or incorporating diversity and inclusion themes into regular communications and meetings. Leaders who make diversity and inclusion visible and valued help to create a culture where all employees feel welcomed and respected.

Traditional organizations typically have rigidly structured communications channels. In such organizations, it is typical to hear the phrase "chain of command", which is borrowed from military culture. Workers in such environments are counseled to communicate upward in a structured manner, through their next highest manager, and so on. These communication structures tend to frustrate workers because there is a level of trust afforded the managers that the issue is properly represented along the "chain". It also assumes that the message will go forward and not be derailed (intentionally or accidentally). Innovative organizations foster open communication and feedback. To be most effective, leaders should create channels for open, honest communication and feedback, especially around diversity and inclusion issues. This could involve regular town hall meetings, anonymous suggestion boxes, or pulse surveys. Leaders should actively listen to and address employee concerns and be transparent about the actions they are taking to create a more inclusive environment.

Innovative organizations provide mentorship and sponsorship opportunities to their people. Leaders should provide mentorship and sponsorship opportunities to help underrepresented employees advance their careers and access high-visibility projects and roles. This could involve formal mentorship programs, sponsorship initiatives, or leadership development programs targeted at diverse talent. Investing in the development and advancement of diverse employees creates a more equitable and inclusive pipeline of future leaders. In large organizations, career advancement opportunities (e.g., promotions, project assignments, leadership opportunities, etc...) are reviewed and approved by corporate boards composed of organizational leaders. The sponsoring of underrepresented personnel in these boards is critical for them to receive due consideration for the career advancing opportunities (Brown, 2022).

Promoting diversity and inclusion is an ongoing journey that requires commitment, transparency, and accountability from leaders at all levels. Taking proactive steps to address inequities, foster belonging, and celebrate diversity drives innovation forward.

CHAPTER 9

Aligning Values, Policies, and Practices with Innovation

"Your work is going to fill a large part of your life, and the only way to be truly satisfied is to do what you believe is great work."

—Steve Jobs

ligning organizational values, policies, and practices with innovation is crucial for creating a culture where innovation can thrive and be sustained over time. "If the functional innovation strategy is not aligned with the overall business strategy this process and these resources will not be able contribute successfully to achieving the overall company goals and objectives" (Katz, Du Preez and Schutte, 2011). When innovation is seen as a natural extension of the organization's values and ways of working, it becomes more palatable and less threatening to those who may be resistant to change.

Innovation comes in many forms and with numerous definitions, so organizational leaders need to make it more acceptable to the workforce by aligning innovation initiatives to the organizational values, policies and practices. Embedding innovation into the organization's values and communicating it clearly creates a shared understanding of what innovation means and why it's important. This helps to demystify innovation and make it feel more accessible and relevant to employees across the organization. Once there is an understanding of the role of innovation within the organization, people need to understand how it works in the organizational decision space. A framework for decision-making that considers innovation needs to be well understood. When innovation is aligned with organizational values, it provides a clear framework for decision-making at all levels (Katz, Du Preez and Schutte, 2011). Employees can use the values as a guide for determining which ideas and initiatives to pursue, and leaders can use them to prioritize and allocate resources. This helps to ensure that innovation efforts are consistent and strategically aligned.

Supporting innovation efforts when traditional efforts are being pursued can be challenging, but if properly addressed, both tracks can complement each other. A seemingly constant refrain about innovation efforts is inflexible budget processes. Rather than traditionally fixed budget cycles, to enable innovation, the organization must implement rolling budgets or innovation funds outside traditional cycles. Remember that innovation efforts are responding to the strategic goals of the organization, and this may cause disruptions to existing lines of business as resources are shared between the two tracks. The organization must develop a risk management approach balancing safe and bold initiatives. Innovation efforts may require out of cycle procurement of resources. Fast-track processes for innovation-related purchases and partnerships are necessary to evaluate ideas or to fabricate prototypes. While traditional corporate pursuits are compliant by design, innovation efforts may not initially be compliant or may require the establishment of new and updated policies to enable and accelerate innovation, not hinder it. Regularly review and adjust policies with an innovation lens.

Once innovation concepts are understood and the mechanism for its governance is put into place, this creates an innovation framework that reinforces desired behaviors. Organizational policies and practices can be powerful tools for reinforcing the behaviors and mindsets that support innovation. For example, performance management systems that reward risk-taking and learning from failure, or collaboration tools that facilitate cross-functional teamwork, can help to create an environment where innovation is encouraged and supported. Additionally, when leaders consistently demonstrate a commitment to innovation through their actions and decisions, it builds trust and credibility with employees. This is particularly important in organizations where innovation may have been viewed with skepticism or resistance in the past. Leaders who walk the talk and follow through on innovation commitments can help to overcome workforce cynicism and build momentum for change (Cameron, 2020).

Innovative organizations attract and retain innovative talent. Organizations that have a strong reputation for innovation are more likely to attract and retain top talent who value creativity, experimentation, and continuous learning. Ensuring the alignment of corporate values, policies, and practices with innovation creates a compelling employee value proposition that sets them apart in the marketplace. In addition to attracting and retaining innovative talent, innovative organizations engender customer and stakeholder trust. When organizations consistently demonstrate a commitment to innovation, it can enhance trust and credibility with customers and other external stakeholders. This is particularly important in industries where innovation is a key driver of competitiveness and differentiation. Aligning innovation activities with organizational values, companies can build a strong brand identity and reputation for leadership. Aligning values, policies, and practices with innovation is critical for long-term sustainability (Yang and Hsu, 2010). In today's rapidly changing business environment, organizations that can continuously innovate and adapt are more likely to survive and thrive over time. Leaders who make innovation a core part of the organization's DNA ensure that it remains a priority even as market conditions and leadership change.

To effectively align organizational values, policies, and practices with innovation, leaders should clearly articulate the organization's innovation values and communicate them widely to all employees. These values should be specific, memorable, and actionable. Another leadership consideration is to conduct comprehensive reviews of organizational policies and practices to identify areas where they may be misaligned with innovation (Yang and Hsu, 2010). Leaders should commit to updating these policies and practices to support and encourage innovative behaviors and mindsets. Leaders at all levels of the organization should model the behaviors and mindsets that support innovation, such as curiosity, risk-taking, and collaboration. They should also be transparent about their own learning and growth.

The organization must routinely celebrate and reward innovation. This includes regularly celebrating and rewarding employees and teams that demonstrate innovative thinking and outcomes. This could involve public recognition, bonuses, or other incentives. To this end, the organization should establish clear metrics and Key Performance Indicators (KPIs) for innovation and regularly track and report on progress. This data should be used to identify areas for improvement and celebrate successes. Using a holistic approach to align values, policies, and practices with innovation, organizations create and reinforces a culture where innovation is embraced, supported, and sustained over time.

CHAPTER 10

Designing Physical and Virtual Workspaces

"Innovation comes from people meeting up in the hallways or calling each other at 10:30 at night with a new idea."

—Steve Jobs

I n today's increasingly distributed and remote work environments, designing physical and virtual workspaces that inspires creativity, and collaboration is more important than ever (Nabergoj and Uršič, 2024). When employees are not co-located, it can be challenging to foster the kind of spontaneous interactions, serendipitous connections, and collaborative energy that often fuel innovation. However, with intentional design and the right tools and strategies, organizations can create workspaces that bridge the distance and support innovation. This topic was briefly touched upon in the earlier chapter when the topic of experimentation was discussed, but more focus is provided to address the means of creating the holistic environment for enabling innovation to flourish.

Within the sphere of innovation, the proposed idea topics of exploration can vary wildly, so the environment must be capable of supporting and enabling numerous types of pursuits; from simple to wildly complex. This means the hosting organization must think with a mind on the future to anticipate the capabilities to be made available to the innovators who will use the space to create their envisioned innovation. To this end, the organization may wish to create an innovation environment that is flexible and modular, from a physical perspective. For employees who do come into the office, create physical workspaces that are flexible, modular, and designed to support different types of work and collaboration. This could include open collaboration areas, quiet focus zones, and multi-purpose rooms that can be easily reconfigured for different activities (Nabergoj and Uršič, 2024). Use furniture, lighting, and other design elements to create a warm, inviting atmosphere that encourages people to linger and connect.

For remote employees, investing in high-quality virtual collaboration tools that allow for seamless communication and co-creation becomes important to create great innovator experiences. This may include video conferencing software, digital whiteboards, project management platforms, and virtual reality tools that create immersive experiences. Ensure that these tools are easy to use, reliable, and accessible to all employees regardless of location or device. One of the biggest challenges of remote work is the lack of informal, spontaneous interactions that often happen around the water cooler or in the hallway (Biuk-Aghai and Hawryszkiewycz, 1999). To recreate these moments virtually, consider hosting regular virtual coffee chats, happy hours, or other casual gatherings where employees can connect and share ideas in a relaxed setting. Encourage the use of chat and messaging tools for informal check-ins and idea sharing throughout the day. Just as physical workspaces can be designed to inspire creativity; virtual workspaces can be designed to support innovation as well (Rattner, 2019). Consider creating virtual innovation labs or collaboration spaces where employees can come together to brainstorm, prototype, and test ideas (Biuk-Aghai and Hawryszkiewycz, 1999). These spaces could include virtual whiteboards, 3D modeling tools, and other creative tools that allow for real-time co-creation and experimentation.

Encourage cross-functional collaboration: In a distributed work environment, it can be easy for employees to become siloed within their own teams or departments. To encourage cross-functional collaboration, consider creating virtual communities of practice or interest groups around specific topics or challenges. Encourage employees to join these groups and share their perspectives and ideas, regardless of their formal role or location. To ensure that employees are able to effectively use virtual collaboration tools and engage in remote innovation activities, provide ongoing training and support (Biuk-Aghai and Hawryszkiewycz, 1999). This could include virtual workshops on design thinking, agile methodologies, or other innovation frameworks, as well as technical training on specific tools and platforms. Ensure that employees have access to the resources and support they need to be successful in a remote work environment.

As mentioned earlier, innovation activities must be routinely showcased and celebrated across the organization, regardless of where it originates. Use virtual town halls, newsletters, or other communication channels to share stories of successful innovations and the teams behind them. Encourage employees to share their own innovation journeys and learnings and create opportunities for cross-pollination and inspiration across the organization.

Designing physical and virtual workspaces that inspire creativity, and collaboration requires a holistic approach that considers the needs and preferences of all employees, regardless of location (Nijhawan, 2020). Creating flexible, engaging spaces and providing the tools and support needed for effective virtual collaboration fosters a culture of innovation that transcends physical distance. As remote and hybrid work continue to evolve, organizations that prioritize the design of their workspaces are better positioned to attract and retain top talent, drive innovation, and adapt to the changing world of work.

PART III

Empowering People for Innovation

CHAPTER 11

Identifying and Developing Innovators

"The best way to predict the future is to create it."

—Peter Drucker

dentifying and developing innovation advocates, sponsors, and champions at various levels of the organization is crucial for driving a culture of innovation and ensuring that new ideas and initiatives have the support and resources they need to succeed.

An Innovation Champion is typically defined as an informal role that exists at the middle management level who drives specific innovation projects or initiatives. The Innovation Champion may take on responsibilities of leading innovation efforts from concept to implementation, but from a management perspective. The efforts may be localized to a specific internal business unit or span several internal business units as cross-functional team efforts. The innovation champion helps to overcome indifference and any resistance to the innovation. Ideas offered that may lead to an eventual innovation must have a champion or will likely not succeed (Howell and Higgins, 1990).

The Innovator represents the hands-on level of innovation within an organization. It embodies the concept that anyone, regardless of their position, can contribute innovative ideas. This role aligns well with the emphasis on fostering a culture of innovation throughout the entire organization. The innovator role provides a contrast to more formal innovation roles like Innovation Champions or Sponsors. This distinction touts the notion that innovation isn't just the responsibility of those in designated positions but can come from any employee with a good idea and the passion to pursue it. The innovator reinforces the empowerment of employees in contributing to corporate innovation goals. The role illustrates how organizations can tap into the creativity and problem-solving abilities of their entire workforce, not just those in leadership or designated innovation roles. The journey of an innovator, from having an initial idea to potentially seeing it implemented, provides a concrete example of how innovation processes can work in practice. The innovator role illustrates how a culture of innovation can transform an organization by encouraging employees to step out of their comfort zones and contribute ideas. This aligns with the book's focus on cultural change as a key driver of innovation. While there are several innovation roles discussed, the innovator serves a unique function that complements rather than redundantly overlaps with other roles.

These roles play different but complimentary functions in the innovation ecosystem, and it's important to have a mix of all three to create a robust and sustainable innovation culture.

While organizations can exercise their prerogative to hire exter-nal innovators, to establish and grow a true culture of innovation requires continual engagement of the workforce. The only way to achieve this goal is to grow the innovation mindset internally. Taking such an approach means that the organization must invest heavily in its people to educate them on innovation princi-ples and train them on innovation methods and processes they can use to advance the bottom line of the organization (Michaelis and Markham, 2017).

Innovation advocates are passionate about innovation and are often the first to embrace new ideas and ways of working. They may be found at any level of the organization, from entry-level employees to senior leaders. What are the characteristics of innovation advocates? To identify potential advocates, look for individuals who consistently generate and share new ideas and seem to possess an insatiable curiosity and appetite for learn-ing. These people have little tolerance for rules that do not make sense for advancing the interests of the organization. To that end, they embrace change and are willing to take risks to get better results than the status quo.

Innovation advocates tend to collaborate well with others and exercise their propensity to build strong and productive rela-tionships. Such people are a force to be reckoned with and they typically have strong track records of implementing innovative solutions in their respective work.

Organizations can use a variety of methods to identify poten-tial advocates, including innovation challenges, hackathons, and employee surveys that ask about innovation interests and experi-ences. Once identified, provide advocates with training, resources, and opportunities to lead innovation initiatives and inspire others.

Innovation advocates are more than enthusiasts who stand on the periphery cheering for the people involved in the daily pursuit of innovations. They may become active participants in the process. In fact, many of them may have desires to create "working examples" by engaging as an innovator and pursuing ideas through the established innovation process. Innovation advocates typically exude positivity within the workforce, and they actively engage and encourage people to step into the innovation space and help define a new and exciting future for the organization.

Innovation sponsors are senior leaders who have the authority and influence to allocate resources and remove barriers to innovation. They play a critical role in championing innovation at the executive level and ensuring that it remains a strategic priority. To develop innovation sponsors, organizations should educate senior leaders on the business case for innovation and its impact on key metrics. Leaders must be able to make value-based decisions and have to develop an understanding of the potential impact on their respective portfolios and the larger impact on the business enterprise. One way to educate senior leaders and enlist their sponsorship of corporate innovation is to provide executive training on innovation leadership and sponsorship best practices. The training should provide the theory behind corporate innovation but also include hands-on and minds-on experiences to reinforce the concepts and to build competence in leading an innovative organization.

Senior leaders should be encouraged to serve as mentors or advisors to innovation teams to experience what it is like to participate in an innovation pursuit so that the leaders gain a first-hand appreciation of the process, the potential gain in satisfying the enterprise goals and the growth of corporate knowledge and experience. They may also realize the positive impact on the workforce culture and trust that ideas from workforce may be as impactful as those ideas generated within the c-suite. Leaders should be recognized and rewarded for consistently sponsoring and supporting innovation. At the same time, they should be held accountable for innovation outcomes as part of their performance metrics.

Innovation champions are the bridge between advocates and sponsors and play a key role in driving innovation projects forward and building buy-in and support across the organization. They are often mid-level leaders who have a deep understanding of both the technical and business aspects of innovation. To cultivate innovation champions, organizations should identify high-potential employees with a track record of leading successful projects. While such individuals may be awesome at yielding great results they must be given the requisite training on innovation methodologies, change management, and influencing skills to be as successful using the newer innovative approaches.

Innovation champions are assigned to lead high-priority innovation initiatives with executive sponsorship. Because they work on corporately sanctioned efforts, they are encouraged to create a community of practice for champions to share knowledge and best practices and support each other. As with all other innovation roles within the organization, Innovation Champions should be recognized and rewarded for their contributions to innovation, both financially and non-financially.

Recall the distinctions between the roles of Innovation Champions and innovators, in the context of internal corporate innovation activities. Typically, Innovation Champions are those people who take on the responsibility to lead corporately sanctioned innovation-themed efforts. They are entrusted with the leadership of such efforts that have corporate sponsorship. An innovator, however, typically works at a grassroots level to pursue an idea that is believed to have potential positive impact on the organization's bottom-line goals. Both roles are important to help the organization reach its strategic goals while encouraging employees to put forth their own ideas that align with corporate goals and pursue them as potential innovations.

To produce the next big thing that gets everyone excited, ideas are required. Ideas spring forth from people who have developed a need for something different, useful or that addresses an emerging issue. To get those ideas from the minds of people who have been thinking about the needs and possible solutions requires them to be compelled to offer their thoughts, opinions, and approaches. People need to feel like they will be heard, and their ideas considered before they, in general, would be willing to offer them as potential ways to solve known or emerging problems.

To extract those potentially brilliant ideas from people who may hold the key to the next big thing, relationships must be formed between the organization and the individuals that are aligned with the organization. The relationship between the person and the organization could be that of an employee (internal) or as a customer/partner (external). So, before future technical outcomes can be achieved the innovation advocates and champions must interact with people in the workforce from a social perspective.

People are comfortable in the midst of crowds. In this context, the workforce and its culture represent the crowd. Their identity is tied to the crowd and if they conform to the norms of the crowd, they do not stand out as individuals or leaders. They are merely unidentifiable members of the herd. People who have been working in an organization in specific roles have an appreciation for their respective jobs. They also have ideas about how to make their work more meaningful and perhaps more efficient. To have their ideas considered would be great but those ideas, if implemented, might change the way the organization produces products or delivers services. Individuals must step out of the crowd and suggest ideas that may cause slight or immense change. This act of stepping away from the comfort and thinking of the crowd is key to beginning the innovation process.

The initial step of a person breaking away from the crowd and overcoming the urge to merely blend into the fabric of the crowd to trusting that they can make a difference. As people formulate and offer innovation ideas, they distinguish themselves as more than unidentifiable members of a crowd. Putting forth an idea signals that they are making a bold statement that there is something better than the status quo. Also, by emerging from the crowd to put forth an idea, they become a driving force for innovation as *idea contributors.*

As an idea contributor, they are distinguishing themselves by both stepping out of the crowd and stepping toward an innovation venue that offers an opportunity to refine, and stress test the idea and perhaps grow it into an innovation.

The passion about the idea motivated the idea contributor to offer an idea to the innovation venue, but that may not be the end of the journey for that person. The people in the innovation venue have a great understanding about how ideas become future innovations. That process requires a person who believes in the idea and wants to see it succeed. Although the idea contributor offered the idea the likelihood that someone else would instantly latch on and support and potentially enable the idea is unrealistic. So, what is the next step?

Once the idea contributor understands that nobody will be as passionate about their idea than themselves, the deal may be closing in on success. Innovation coaches are key to this conversion process from idea contributor to an innovator. They walk the idea contributor through a step-by-step process to lower the level of anxiety being felt by the contributor. Finally, a breakthrough occurs, and the idea contributor says "yes"! At that point, the idea contributor is instantaneously converted to an innovator and will enjoy all the rights, privileges, and challenges, thereof.

An offered idea has the best opportunity of becoming an innovation only if the energy applied to its success is driven by the passion of the idea contributor. The innovation venue people must make a convincing case for the idea contributor to take on this role. They must convince the person that this idea stands the best chance if the idea contributor engages in the process to ensure the best opportunity for success. If the idea contributor is convinced by the argument that person is converted into an *innovator* and takes on an exciting set of responsibilities and could potentially be a major catalyst for positive change!

Every innovation is the product of an initial idea, the passion of the person who wants to see it succeed (e.g. a champion) and a process that identifies and resolves risks to increase its odds of becoming a big hit. The innovation is a manifestation of numerous conversations, arguments and agreements occurring around ideas that are offered and pursued. Breaking away from the status quo, putting forth an idea, taking on the responsibilities and challenges of pursuing something new is exciting and rewarding, but innovation does not occur in isolation. The process of creating the desired change through an innovation process requires transforming the mindset of people in the crowd to play an active role in taking their ideas from conception through fruition. This social engagement is necessary to create innovators. Innovators play a critical role in any innovation process.

Developing a strong network of innovation advocates, sponsors, and champions is not a one-time event, but an ongoing process that requires continued investment and support. To keep these key players engaged and effective, organizations should continuously provide regular training and development opportunities, including exposure to external thought leaders and best practices (Michaelis and Markham, 2017). Organizational leaders should look for and create opportunities for advocates, sponsors, and champions to collaborate and learn from each other. The corporation must make a point to highlight, celebrate and share the successes and learnings of innovation initiatives across the organization. As mentioned previously, the people serving in the various innovation roles may change over time. In fact, they should be encouraged to do so to keep the ideas fresh and to grow innovation expertise by having others take on these roles to gain greater innovation knowledge and experience. Organizations, therefore, should develop a means to continuously assess and adjust the mix of advocates, sponsors, and champions based on changing business needs and priorities.

Organizations that take a systematic approach to identifying and developing innovation advocates, sponsors, and [innovation and idea] champions can create a powerful engine for driving innovation at all levels (Michaelis and Markham, 2017). These key players can help to create a shared vision and language for innovation, build momentum and buy-in for new ideas, and ensure that innovation remains a strategic priority over the long term. As with any cultural change effort, it requires consistent leadership, communication, and reinforcement to truly take hold, but the payoff in terms of increased agility, competitiveness, and employee engagement can be significant.

CHAPTER 12

Innovation Training and Skill Development

> *"Learning and innovation go hand in hand. The arrogance of success is to think that what you did yesterday will be sufficient for tomorrow."*

—William Pollard

Providing innovation training and skill development opportunities is essential for building a workforce that is capable of driving innovation at all levels of the organization. To make this happen, organizations should take a comprehensive and strategic approach (Michaelis and Markham, 2017). Keep in mind that the current workforce may have limited exposure to innovation concepts and processes so knowledge and skills development may take a considerable amount of time to achieve the levels of competency needed to realize the organizational goals.

Organizations must have clarity on where they exist on the innovation spectrum. They can gain this understanding by conducting an assessment of the current innovation skills and capabilities of the workforce, using tools such as surveys, interviews, and focus groups. Identify the specific skills and knowledge areas that are most critical for innovation in your organization, based on your industry, strategy, and goals. This could include skills such as design thinking, agile methodology, data analysis, or customer empathy. The innovation methodology selected by the organization will influence the type of knowledge and skills training selected for the workforce. Use the assessment results to identify gaps and prioritize areas for training and development.

Based on the identified skills and gaps, develop a comprehensive curriculum of innovation training programs that cover a range of topics and levels. Make certain to include foundational courses on innovation mindsets, behaviors, and processes. This approach will reinforce many of the concepts discussed earlier. In addition to the foundational courses, based on the selected innovation methodology employees will need to engage specialized courses on specific tools and methodologies, such as design thinking or lean startup. For the organizational leadership, advanced courses on innovation leadership, culture, and strategy are necessary to ensure that the innovation goals are central to the thrust to get the workforce innovation efforts are aligned to the organizational strategic goals.

The organization may also wish to incorporate fun and experiential learning opportunities, such as innovation projects or hackathons to spur interest and simultaneously build competence in the appropriate technologies and innovation processes. Such opportunities and events help to promote continuous learning.

Lastly on this point, resources, such as online courses, books, and articles should be made available to members at all levels of the workforce to keep the interest in innovation firmly placed in the minds of the workforce. This ensures that the curriculum is aligned with the organization's values, goals, and processes, and that it is accessible and relevant to employees at all levels and functions.

To accommodate different learning styles and preferences, organizations should consider offering a variety of learning formats and modalities (Sultana, Christ and Meyrueis, 2013). An effective staple in many organizations is the in-person workshops and training sessions format, where experts on specific topics provide detailed knowledge and guidance on topics that have direct benefit to the workforce. Such training opportunities may be costly, depending on the topic and the instructors who are expected to impart rare and high-demand knowledge and skills. Another useful means of acquiring knowledge and skills is the use of online self-paced courses and webinars offered by platforms such as Coursera, Udemy, Udacity and Manning. Many of the courses offered in this format are typically targeted to upskill the learner in a short period of time and on numerous electronic platforms (Sultana, Christ and Meyrueis, 2013).

In addition to the externally available (in-person or online) courses, organizations may also tap internal opportunities to share knowledge through peer learning and mentoring programs . Members of the workforce should be encouraged to share their knowledge and skills, either formally or informally, with peers and subordinate employees (Lee, Yeh, Yu, and Luo, 2023). Such knowledge sharing is helpful at all levels of the workforce. Knowledge sharing and skills development reaches further than on-the-job learning and mentoring but may include stretch assignments, locally or elsewhere within the organization (Lee, Yeh, Yu, and Luo, 2023). Some organizations establish formalized skills cross-training opportunities that are competitive and structured in ways to accelerate the careers of employees who successfully navigate the program.

External conferences and events are useful for employees to participate in for professional development and expansion of their respective networks within their respective categories of interest. As interest grows in the topic of innovation, many conferences and webinars provide insights and forecasts that are essential in helping attendees to envision approaches to solving key industry problems.

Another key trend with forward-thinking organizations is to set up dedicated innovation labs and spaces for experimentation and collaboration (Mollmann, 2023). Spaces may be used by any employee and are outfitted with a range of resources to enable employees to explore their concepts in an informal way. While the innovation labs may be associated with the formalized innovation venue, they may be independently managed such that employees do not feel the potential stress of taking on a more formalized pursuit of their respective ideas.

Book publishing companies such as Manning and O'Reilly offer group discounts to organizations seeking to upskill their respective workforces. Topics are typically technology focused and organizations, via the group discounts, can supplement their employees with printed books and online resources that they can access at any time to help them grasp basic knowledge to gain demonstrable expertise using these resources. Innovative organizations routinely provide a range of learning options, organizations to ensure that all personnel have access to the training and development they need to build their innovation skills and capabilities. In fact, according to the Internal Revenue Code Section 127, "Employers that provide their employees with Section 127 educational assistance benefits can deduct these costs as a business expense in determining their income tax liability" (AAU, 2019).

Organizational leadership must make the move to signal the importance of innovation and ensure that employees have the time and resources to engage in training and development, making it a strategic priority (Hattori and Wycoff, 2004).

Leaders should set aside dedicated time and budget for innovation training and development. This can be incentivized using a variety of means. The bottom line is that it establishes a norm that everyone in the organization is expected and encouraged to innovate. An additional approach to incentivize innovation is to incorporate innovation skills and behaviors into performance goals and reviews and setup a scaled criteria to give employees goals to motivate them to innovate more (Hattori and Wycoff, 2004). When employees take the challenge, they should be rewarded for their efforts. The organization should establish a means of recognizing and rewarding employees who demonstrate innovation skills and leadership. This may include recognition for employees who pursue external training and certifications in areas that are important to the organization. The organization can share innovation news by communicating regularly about the value and impact of innovation training and development.

Finally, it's important to measure and optimize the impact of innovation training and development over time. Organizational leadership must establish a means of measuring the rate of its transformation from a traditional footing to an innovative footing. There are numerous ways for the leadership to better understand how well the organization is making the transition (Misra, 2024). Leadership should have a means of tracking workforce participation and completion rates for training programs. It should also have a means for identifying gross-level numbers of employees who have taken advantage of specific courses and other learning opportunities.

Another common way of assessing changes in employee skills, behaviors, and mindsets is through surveys and assessments. Questions in such surveys must elicit core insights to enable leadership to determine the level of emphasis they must apply to grow the organization's innovation culture. Measuring the impact of innovation training on key business metrics, such as new product revenue or customer satisfaction is important to assess whether innovation is making a positive impact on the customers.

A key skill of a learning organization is its ability to listen to its workforce and take cues, accordingly. Gathering feedback and ideas from employees on how to improve and evolve the training curriculum is critically important (Misra, 2024). Information of this type can ensure the continuous updating and adapting of the training curriculum based on changing needs and priorities. Using a data-driven and iterative approach to innovation training and development helps organizations to ensure that they are getting the most value and impact from their investments.

Making innovation training and skill development a strategic priority and providing a comprehensive and diverse curriculum of learning opportunities is essential for building an innovation-capable workforce. Organizations can assess workforce skills and gaps, leverage diverse learning formats and make training a priority. Additionally, they can measure and optimize impact to create an environment of continuous learning and development that drives innovation and competitive advantage.

CHAPTER 13

Cross-functional Collaboration and Knowledge Sharing

"Alone we can do so little; together we can do so much."

—Helen Keller

Encouraging and incentivizing cross-functional collaboration and knowledge sharing is crucial for driving innovation and preventing the loss of valuable organizational knowledge. There are numerous strategies that leadership can use to foster a culture of collaboration and knowledge sharing. The discussion elaborates on some of the ideas that organizations should potentially consider. Before getting into the positive attributes of knowledge sharing, male note of the effects of the opposite behavior of knowledge hiding or concealment (Song,

Yang, Zhang and Huang, 2023). In such cases where knowledge is concealed and not shared, there are direct correlations to negative implications of organizational fairness and the inability of workers to perform their respective roles (Song, Yang, Zhang and Huang, 2023). On occasion, illustrating the downsides of an issue further reinforces the rationale to seek a different alternative.

Clearly communicate the importance and benefits of collaboration and knowledge sharing for both individual and organizational success. Emphasize how it can lead to better decision-making, problem-solving, innovation, and career growth. Use case studies and examples to illustrate the positive impact of collaboration and knowledge sharing in action.

Organizations should provide a mix of formal and informal opportunities for employees to collaborate and share knowledge across functions and levels. The idea is to make the work environment more conducive to sharing ideas, project results, lessons learned and other useful information that may be used to inform others in the organization to either avoid or consider incorporating into their current and future work. Cross-functional project teams and working groups offer great opportunities to collaborate and level set the knowledge gained from current or past work to inform future work (Olsson and Bosch, 2016).

Another great way to grow the knowledge base of the organization in distinct categories are communities of practice and interest groups. Although their information may be shared broadly within the larger organization, the knowledge they cultivate is specific to the topic of interest to its members.

On the informal collaboration side of the discussion, events such as lunch and learn sessions and brown bag discussions offer the opportunity for anyone to take the stage to share ideas on a topic of the day or to teach a very specific skill, usually within the timeframe allocated for lunch. If the level of excitement around innovation needs to be cranked up, one way to accomplish this goal is by issuing innovation challenges. This creates a healthy in-house competitive pursuit that enables the winners of the challenge to claim bragging rights. The key is to set the award standard very low such that all participants and onlookers understand that the event is just for fun, and no judgement is cast on any of the participants.

One way to strengthen the organizational culture is to spend more time with members of the workforce. Social events and team-building activities are great ways to grow the culture in more relaxed settings where people can learn about and gain a better understanding of how their co-workers think and to gain an appreciation for their respective interests and motivations. The creation of multiple touchpoints and forums for collaboration, organizations can make it easier and more natural for employees to connect and share knowledge (Olsson and Bosch, 2016).

Invest in tools and platforms (i.e., scaffolding) that support collaboration and knowledge sharing. Organizations investing in innovation often overlook the necessary scaffolding that must be put in place to enable the more effective means of helping to take ideas from the point of inception to the final realization. The evidence of this reality is the use of office automation tooling to support nearly every facet of the innovation process. While convenient, office automation tooling does not generally address the needs of the entire innovation process; no matter the innovation methodologies adopted by the organization.

Ideally, the innovation scaffolding selected to enable innovation should be specific to the methodology and to the organizational goals. If the methodology is incompatible with the manner in which the organization wants to operate, the organization will have to adapt to the constraints of the methodology rather than the other way around. The innovation scaffolding should share compatibilities such that data created by the various tools. In short, the innovation scaffolding should form an innovation ecosystem of interoperable tools and data that can perform the full functionality of the chosen innovation methodology. Some useful capabilities to implement as a part of the scaffolding might include the following:

✦ Collaboration software and project management tools,
✦ Knowledge management systems and wikis,
✦ Enterprise social networks and chat platforms,
✦ Video conferencing and virtual meeting tools,
✦ Idea management and innovation platforms,
✦ Performance management and assessment tools and
✦ Report generation tools.

Few organizations can afford the expense of building innovation methodology-specific tooling to support their goals (Olsson and Bosch, 2016). More realistically speaking, organizations can identify commercial tooling that can interoperate to compose the innovation scaffolding necessary to meet their requirements. The organization must ensure that these tools are user-friendly, accessible, and integrated with existing workflows and processes. The organization must provide training and support to help employees effectively use these tools for collaboration and knowledge sharing.

The innovation scaffolding capabilities, the physical and virtual innovation venues, the participating organizations and the people engaged in any facet of the innovation process constitutes the organization's innovation ecosystem. Within the innovation eco-system, the organization should be able to create the conditions for any member of the organization to innovate and expand the organization's ability to be competitive in their chosen market.

Recognize and reward employees who consistently demon-strate collaborative behaviors and contribute to knowledge sharing (McKinney, 2023). Placing emphasis on outward appre-ciation for those members of the workforce involved in innovation activities serves to further instill the values of organization in its workforce. While traditional organizations celebrate the "success" as the completion of a project, for instance, those people involved in the innovation activities may be recognized for a variety of milestones or even their participation. Public recognition and praise in team meetings or company events, for instance, serves to inculcate the value of innovation to the organization and this strengthens the organization's innovation culture.

There are numerous ways the organization can recognize its people for their involvement for participating and furthering the bottom-line innovation goals. Bonuses, gift cards, or other financial incentives are always welcomed by employees of the organiza-tion, but there are additional means of recognizing people. The organization leadership may wish to start and "Innovator of the Month" designation to bestow on a worthy person that is nomi-nated by their peers, for instance.

To further incentivize the workforce to embrace and opt into the organization's innovation culture, the leadership may adver-tise that active innovation participants will benefit by becoming priority nominees for opportunities for professional development and growth. They may also receive consideration in perfor-mance reviews and promotions as a means of accelerating their respective careers within the organization. Organizations should encourage, celebrate and reward collaboration and knowledge sharing to signal its importance and enable employees to engage in these behaviors.

Senior leaders and managers must model collaborative behaviors and knowledge sharing in their own work. This is especially important because the workforce needs to see visual confirmation that the leadership is serious about transforming the organization's traditional culture to an innovation culture. Such commitment by the leadership is critical to create an atmosphere of innovation unity that spans across leadership and the workforce (RLG, 2018).

In such an environment, leaders must actively seek out input and feedback from other functions and levels. This behavior indicates that organizational leadership values its people and their thoughts and ideas. Leaders should also make a point of sharing their own knowledge and expertise through mentoring, blogging, or presenting. The workforce needs to know they have the attention of leadership and that their contributions are valued. This may be evidenced when leaders routinely engage in or kick-off cross-functional projects and initiatives. During such activities, leaders may take part in recognizing and celebrating the collaborative successes of their teams (RLG, 2018). When leaders consistently demonstrate the value of collaboration and knowledge sharing, it can have a powerful trickle-down effect on the rest of the organization (Gardner, 2017).

Organizations that produce tangible products can easily identify and implement measures to determine how well they are doing by observing the number of products manufactured over some defined period of time. Within the innovation sphere, however, assessing the effectiveness of the organization might not be as apparent. As the innovation culture matures, however, the knowledge gained and shared are likely indicators that deserve some attention. The organization, therefore, must establish metrics and Key Performance Indicators (KPIs) to track the effectiveness of collaboration and knowledge sharing initiatives (World at Work, 2022). Such measure should include but are not limited to the following essential elements:

✦ **Workforce Engagement** – May be used to track participation rates in collaboration opportunities and platforms. This may consist of measures that track such things as the number of active users on collaboration platforms, the frequency of interactions (posts, comments, likes, shares), or time spent on collaboration platforms (El Bassiti and Ajhoun, 2016).

✦ **Contributions** - Number and quality of ideas generated through cross-functional collaboration. This may consist of measures such as the number of new knowledge assets created (documents, articles, videos), the quality of knowledge assets (ratings, feedback, usefulness), and the diversity of contributors across departments and levels (Olsson and Bosch, 2016).

✦ **Employee Experience Index** - Employee satisfaction and engagement scores related to collaboration and knowledge sharing are important within the organization because the ability of the organization to continually meet its goals and remain competitive (World at Work, 2022). An index instrument may be constructed to measure perceived value of collaboration and knowledge sharing (collected via surveys), increased employee retention and reduced turnover and improved onboarding time for new employees.

✦ **Business Impact** – Business outcomes and ROI of collaborative projects and initiatives. This measure may track cost savings from reduced duplication of efforts, increased productivity and efficiency and improved time-to-market for new products or services (El Bassiti and Ajhoun, 2016).

These KPIs represent a subset of the types of measures that would provide useful insights to help organizational leaders best understand how well knowledge sharing is occurring across the corporate enterprise. Leaders can use the insights to identify areas for improvement and optimize collaboration and knowledge sharing strategies over time. It is important to choose KPIs that align with the organization's specific goals and priorities, and to regularly review and adjust them as needed.

Encouraging and incentivizing cross-functional collaboration and knowledge sharing requires a multi-faceted approach that includes communication, opportunities, tools, recognition, leadership, measurement, and barrier-busting. Collaboration and knowledge sharing must be a strategic priority and embedding it into the fabric of the organization. When leaders tap into the collective intelligence and expertise of their workforce, it helps them to drive innovation, performance, and growth.

CHAPTER 14

Implementing Effective Idea Management

"Ideas are like rabbits. You get a couple and learn how to handle them, and pretty soon you have a dozen."

—John Steinbeck

mplementing effective idea generation and evaluation processes that engage the entire workforce is essential for driving innovation and tapping into the collective creativity of the organization. This chapter presents some suggested approaches that organizations can take to establish a robust idea generation and evaluation framework (Keko, Jan Prevo and Stremersch, 2017).

Start by defining a clear and compelling business challenge or problem statement that aligns with the organization's strategic priorities and goals (Keko, Jan Prevo and Stremersch, 2017). The challenge should be specific enough to provide focus and direction, but broad enough to allow for diverse ideas and perspectives. Communicate the challenge widely and frequently to the entire organization, emphasizing the importance of everyone's participation and contribution. Challenges serve as a framework to communicate to the workforce that help is needed in specific areas of the business. Such messages tend to focus innovation ideas on the business needs of the larger organization (World at Work, 2022). The challenges should not be so specific that they constrain thoughts that may come from the workforce. If they work properly, however, they will generate ideas that broaden the potential solution space.

Ideas are the fuel that drives the organization's innovation engine. The organization must provide the means to request ideas from the workforce and offer incentives to increase the likelihood of participation. One way to assist in the idea generation and capture process is to offer multiple channels and platforms for employees to submit their ideas. One of the best means of gathering innovation ideas from the workforce is called crowdsourcing. Simply put, the workforce becomes the crowd that routinely contributes ideas that may spur a pursuit to take place within the organization's innovation venue.

Whether the organization is relatively small or huge is size, a technology assist is recommended to capture ideas and comments from the crowd. The technology may be as simple as a website that incorporates a database to capture submitted ideas, reflect the ideas back to the crowd to get feedback and to have the crowd vote in favor or against submitted ideas (WAZOKU, 2018). Such a process involves the entire crowd (i.e., the workforce) and this helps to narrow the potential selection of ideas that are considered for eventual innovation pursuits.

The organization must ensure that the submission process is simple, user-friendly, and accessible to all employees, regardless of their location, function, or level.

Actively encouraging diversity and inclusion in the idea generation process by inviting participation from all functions, levels and backgrounds works to the build trust and enthusiasm within the workforce. The organization must make routine announcements to encourage workforce participation using inclusive language and imagery in communications and promotions. Leaders must insist on providing accommodations and support for employees with different needs or abilities to send a message to the entire organization that every member of the organization is welcomed and encouraged to participate

(WAZOKU, 2018). As an outreach activity from the innovation venue, internal groups and individual employees may be offered training and resources on inclusive idea generation and brainstorming techniques. Fostering a culture of diversity and inclusion in idea generation, organizations helps to generate and expand a wider range of novel and valuable ideas.

Develop clear and transparent criteria and processes for evaluating and selecting ideas for further development and implementation. Are the votes cast by the crowd going to independently select the ideas that move forward, or will the votes determine which ideas are nominated to be further assessed? The criteria should align with the organization's innovation strategy and goals and with strategic priorities and customer needs. The innovation venue should include a small team of idea evaluators who will make decisions about the submitted ideas in accordance with the organization's published criteria(Sandström and Björk, 2009). The process should be transparent, and the crowd should always be able to inquire about the disposition of every submitted idea through the crowd-facing website. The key responsibility for the organization is to communicate the criteria and processes clearly to all employees and ensure that the evaluation team includes diverse representatives from different functions and levels.

Providing timely and constructive feedback to all employees who submit ideas, regardless of whether their ideas are selected for further development is essential (Sandström and Björk, 2009). The feedback should acknowledge the effort and creativity of the employee and provide specific suggestions for improvement or alternative approaches. This type of recognition reinforces the innovation culture's value system of celebrating participation as opposed to only final success. Members of the crowd who further distinguish themselves by contributing ideas are dubbed "contributors" and through their idea contributions help the organization achieve its goals. The contributors may receive public acknowledgement and praise in team meetings or organization communications. They may also be given small tokens of appreciation, such as gift cards or branded merchandise. Contributors are the people most passionate about the ideas they contribute. The innovation venue personnel make it a priority to offer opportunities for contributors to become "innovators" and present and develop their ideas further within the innovation process. Providing feedback and recognition is essential for organizations to encourage continued participation and engagement in the idea generation process.

Within the innovation domain, ideas drive the processes that can potentially result in an innovation. As technology advancement and business environments change, however, the value of ideas may diminish over time. That is the reason that the notion of an idea lifecycle must be established to keep the most relevant and highest potential ideals to be available for consideration while other ideas are taken out of circulation within the organization. Notionally, the ideas are conceived, captured, tagged, refined, assessed, scrutinized and transformed into innovations. If not selected, at some point, ideas are retired and then archived for historical purposes.

Such an idea management framework is necessary to ensure that the most relevant and highest potential ideas are considered, and others are not. Effective idea management supports ideas through each stage, ensuring valuable concepts don't get lost and learnings are captured even from unrealized ideas (Sandström and Björk, 2009).

For the ideas that are selected for further development, the organization must provide the necessary resources and support to bring them to fruition. The majority of this work should be managed under the leadership of the innovation venue personnel. The innovation venue takes on the responsibility to translate ideas into innovations with the help of the innovators, coaches and support personnel. For selected ideas, the innovation process will be used to present, resource, de-risk, and potentially adopt as an innovation to add to the organization's products and service offerings.

The organization must dedicate time, budget, and personnel for idea development and testing to ensure that selected ideas are given the best opportunity to be converted into an adopted innovation. Organizational leaders must enable access to customers, partners, and subject matter experts for feedback and collaboration. As new ideas are accepted into the innovation process, so are new people. Core innovation training and coaching on innovation methodologies must be offered so the participants understand the expectations and that every idea will not necessarily become an innovation. The innovation venue personnel will monitor, measure and report the progress of all submitted ideas; whether they survive the process of fail out of the process along the way (Gerlach and Brem, 2018). Investing in idea development and implementation, organizations signal to the workforce the value and importance of employee-driven innovation.

Implementing effective idea generation and evaluation processes that engage the entire workforce requires a multi-faceted approach that includes clear challenges, multiple submission channels, diversity and inclusion, transparent evaluation criteria, feedback and recognition, investment in development and implementation, and continuous improvement (Gerlach and Brem, 2018). Making idea generation and evaluation a core part of the organization's innovation culture serves to build trust between leadership and employees.

CHAPTER 15

Recognizing and Rewarding Innovative Contributions

"The way to get good ideas is to get lots of ideas and throw the bad ones away."

—Linus Pauling

Recognizing and rewarding innovative contributions is a critical component of fostering a culture of innovation within an organization. To effectively revamp the recognition and rewards strategy, several key considerations must be taken into account. The recognition and rewards system should be aligned with the organization's overall innovation goals and values (World at Work, 2022). This means rewarding behaviors and outcomes that contribute to the organization's innovation priorities.

Generating and implementing novel and valuable ideas is one way for employees to contribute to the innovation goals of the organization while distinguishing themselves in the process. In fact, creative ideas that have the potential to positively impact the bottom-line of the organization should be recognized in meaningful ways. Contributors can be given an identification code within the organization such that they can get credit for their respective contributions. This could be done in the same fashion that is used by the U.S. Patent and Trademark Office (USPTO) in identifying inventors who submit their work for patent consideration. Credits accumulated by each contributor, for example, may be used to purchase items in the organization's gift shop or a partner shop in the local shopping mall. Of course, this is just a creative example of what may be considered for recognition of contributors and others involved in the innovative processes (Al Darmaki and Ismail, 2019).

A dominant trait of all innovators is the habit of taking calculated risks and learning from failures. There is a resilient nature in people who do not quit in the face of failure. They try harder and try to solve problems using different approaches. Innovators are very determined people, and they routinely demonstrate curiosity, creativity, and continuous improvement. Their behavior is contagious, and it causes others around them to behave similarly, and this collective behavior delivers measurable business impact and value.

By clearly communicating and reinforcing the link between rewards and innovation goals, organizations can motivate and engage employees to contribute their best ideas and efforts.

In a culture of innovation, it is important to recognize and reward not just successful innovations, but also the learning and growth that comes from failure. This means celebrating and sharing the lessons learned from failed experiments or projects and recognizing the courage and initiative of employees who take calculated risks, even if they don't pay off. Efforts to find new and viable solutions to problems is a process that creates knowledge along the way. Change the mantra of "tried and failed" to "tried and learned". This mantra will be true even if the desired outcome is achieved. The organization as a whole grows more knowledgeable and capable with every exploration of an idea.

The organization must make it an innovation cultural value of providing opportunities for employees to share their failures and receive feedback and support. There should be no stigma involved with anyone in the organization who devotes their time and energy to help the organization to grow by pursuing an idea to meet the organization's strategic goals. This is the reason that reframing failure as a necessary step in the innovation process, rather than a personal or professional shortcoming.

Recognizing that success requires failure helps organizations to reframe failure as a key requirement to achieve innovation success. This concept helps to create safe environments where employees feel empowered to take risks and learn from their mistakes.

People are unique as it pertains to how they get excited and gain energy to drive forward. This is true in how they like to be recognized. Effective recognition and rewards systems should include a mix of intrinsic and extrinsic motivators. Intrinsic rewards are those that come from the inherent satisfaction and enjoyment of the work itself, such as opportunities for learning, growth, and mastery within the sphere of innovation (Al Darmaki and Ismail, 2019). To assist in such endeavors, many organizations with internal innovation venues, staff the innovation roles with volunteers from the workforce. The innovation roles all have limited terms, and the terms are staggered such that there is never a complete turnover of staff at any given time. This provides continuity of process knowledge and affords innovators a consistent experience when pursuing an innovation idea. Rotating the innovation role assignments enables more members of the workforce to be introduced to the innovation concepts, the venue, the roles and responsibilities and this expands the knowledge and grows the culture of innovation within the organization.

Another way to entice employees to engage in the innovation process is to provide them with a greater level of autonomy and ownership over projects and decisions. Given that innovation processes may differ greatly from the traditional processes within the organization, innovators should be allowed to find new means of getting results. Such pursuits may lead to greater gains in efficiency and more unique products and services to distinguish the organization from its competitors. Such intellectual and operational degrees of freedom provide an increased sense of purpose and contribution to the organization's mission. Employees who engage in the innovation process may also receive peer recognition and feedback that elevates their professional stature as a proven innovator.

Extrinsic rewards, on the other hand, are those that come from external sources, such as bonuses, raises, and promotions and public recognition and awards (Al Darmaki and Ismail, 2019). Such honors are bestowed on innovators by the organization in recognition or their innovative contributions.

Employees venturing into the innovation sphere may be incentivized as they may gain increased access to new opportunities and resources as a result of them stepping out of their traditional roles to take on an innovation challenge that may benefit the larger organization. Offering a mix of intrinsic and extrinsic rewards appeals to the diverse motivations and preferences of their employees (World at Work, 2022).

One size does not fit all when it comes to recognition and rewards. What motivates and engages one employee may not work for another. To maximize the impact of rewards, organizations might consider gathering input and feedback from employees on their preferred forms of recognition and reward. Based on information gained from the employees, the organization may choose to tailor rewards to the individual recipient's career stage, personal goals, and lifestyle. The organization may also choose to offer a menu of reward options that employees can choose from, based on their needs and preferences (Al Darmaki and Ismail, 2019). To avoid the awards and recognition events getting stale, the organization should commit to regularly review and adjust rewards based on changing employee and business needs. Tailoring rewards to individual preferences and needs, organizations can demonstrate their commitment to employee well-being and satisfaction.

To be effective, recognition and rewards should be:

✦ **Timely:** The presentation of the award or recognition should occur as close to the desired behavior or outcome as possible. As soon as a result or milestone is achieved, the innovator should be recognized for the accomplishment. This way the innovator's motivation remains high because their work is seen as valuable to the organization.

✦ **Specific:** The reward should be clearly linked to the innovation contribution or achievement (Al Darmaki and Ismail, 2019). Award and recognition categories are recommended such that they represent the best possible choice that is commensurate with the innovator's achievement or contribution.

✦ **Meaningful:** Any reward presented to the innovator must demonstrate genuine appreciation and value for the employee's efforts (World at Work, 2022). The innovator must see value in the award or recognition and the reward should set the innovator apart from others.

✦ **Personalized:** Rewards should be tailored to the individual's preferences and relationship with the reward giver (World at Work, 2022). Putting the name of the innovator on the award or by giving a token of appreciation that is known to the workforce as a coveted token, the innovator is more likely to place more value on the reward.

✦ **Equitable:** The organization must ensure that all employees have equal opportunities for recognition and reward within the organization as it pertains to innovation.

Making recognition timely, specific, and meaningful, organizations can reinforce the behaviors and outcomes that drive innovation and engagement.

Finally, organizations should measure and communicate the impact of their recognition and rewards system on innovation outcomes and employee engagement. This could be implemented in a variety of ways, but any implementation must be data driven so the organization can engage the proper controls to ensure that rewards are appropriate for the work being performed and that there is opportunity for all employees to be considered for such honors.

Tracking the frequency, diversity, and impact of innovations generated and implemented is a great way to slice the data to analyze the reward trends across the workforce and to spot anomalies that require leadership intervention. Surveying employees on their satisfaction and motivation levels related to rewards and recognition is another means of gathering workforce data concerning their collective experiences as participants and reward recipients based on their respective contributions and final accomplishments. Given that one of the positive attributes of an organization with an innovation culture experiences greater chances of recruiting and retaining talent, that theory should be continually measured by analyzing the retention and performance of employees who receive recognition and rewards. Sharing success stories and case studies of how recognition and rewards have driven innovation and business results is important information to collect and communicate back to the workforce and to place in recruiting messages to prospective employees. Keep in mind that the outreach to prospective employees must consider a multigenerational audience (Opoku and Kwaku Duah, 2019). Shifts in workforce demographics greatly influences the minds of people being sought to fill critical positions in the organization. Appealing to Generation Z (or Gen-Z) represents a radically different approach than what appeals to people aligned with the "Baby Boomer" era. Such considerations may represent a growth opportunity for corporate leaders to better understand and to make the appropriate accommodations to address issues that attract people across the generational spectrum (Opoku and Kwaku Duah, 2019). Most importantly, however, the organization's culture will play a dominant role in the amount of time the newly recruited and hired personnel remain within the organization. Gen-Z employees, for instance, who find their company less agile, in both their thinking and their processes, are more likely to depart to find a company that fosters an agile and experimental culture. Attracting great people who are equipped to contribute in a positive way is a great accomplishment but keeping them, once hired, is essential to the bottom-line work of the organization and for the long-term viability of the organization.

By measuring the impact of rewards, organizations can build a strong case for continued investment in recognition and rewards and inspire ongoing innovation and engagement from their employees.

To build an excited and motivated innovation culture the system of rewards and reinforcement requires new ways to recognize and appreciate participants. In addition to the typical monetary awards, new ways must be explored and implemented.

Organizations can create an Innovation Wall of Fame to showcase innovators and their ideas in a prominent location. In a distributed organization, the wall may be virtualized and placed on the organization's website. Another way an organization can promote a recognition system and reinforce the innovation culture is to inject creativity of making personalized innovation trading cards.

For innovators who get thrills from by getting away to a place where they can think, they may enjoy innovation sabbaticals. Organizations can offer time off to pursue personal innovation projects. While such gestures are focused on the personal interests of the innovator, such opportunities engender trust and loyalty, and the innovators will produce more for the organization that employs them.

Organizations can also create opportunities to host sessions where innovators share their respective journeys. Recognition should be timely, specific, and aligned with the individual's motivations and preferences

Revamping the recognition and rewards strategy for innovation requires aligning rewards with innovation goals, recognizing both success and failure, offering a mix of intrinsic and extrinsic motivators, tailoring rewards to individual preferences, making recognition timely and meaningful, and measuring and communicating the impact of rewards. Considering these factors helps organizations to create a recognition and rewards system that effectively motivates and sustains a culture of innovation.

Supporting Employee Well-being and Work-Life Balance

"The only way to do great work is to love what you do."

—Steve Jobs

Supporting employee well-being and work-life balance is critical for fostering a healthy, engaged, and productive workforce, particularly in the context of innovation. When employees are stressed, burned out, or struggling to manage competing demands, they are less likely to bring their best ideas and efforts to their work. A person's well-being directly affects their ability to contribute to innovative activities to advance the organization's bottom line (Androniceanu, Kinnunen, Georgescu & Androniceanu, 2020). When they are distracted by issues outside the workplace, they are distracted within the workplace. Organizations of all types routinely tout the value of work-life balance but rarely is this idea effectively implemented in a successful way. If organizations wish to grow their respective innovation cultures, they must find ways to make work-life balance a successful endeavor.

One of the most effective ways an organization can support work-life balance is to offer flexible work arrangements (Bello, Tula, Omotoye, Kess-Momoh and Daraojimba, 2024). Flexible hours or compressed work weeks are both excellent ways to give employees more time back to accomplish life goals outside of work. It helps employees better focus when they are performing work for the organization because they can use the flexibility afforded them to handle family or other concerns as needed.

Another way to help create a healthy work-life balance is to offer remote work or telecommuting options. More people are opting to prioritize where they live versus where they work, and this phenomenon has created quite a dilemma for employers. Employees dread the long drive to the office and the joys of being stuck in endless traffic to get to work. Requiring them to be physically present in the office can produce a great amount of stress on the employee and lost productivity for the organization (Bello, Tula, Omotoye, Kess-Momoh and Daraojimba, 2024). The more time the employee spends driving or stuck in traffic, the less time they are focusing on the organization's business goals. Additionally, for geographically dispersed employees, there are opportunities to connect to the corporate environment via the Internet and so that employees can work no matter their location. This also allows the organization to provide service to customers across time zones, so there is mutual benefit for the employees and the organization.

Job sharing or part-time arrangements offer even greater flexibility if employees need to make additional time for themselves and their families. Giving employees more control over when, where, and how they work helps them better manage their personal and professional responsibilities and reduce stress and burnout (Bello, Tula, Omotoye, Kess-Momoh and Daraojimba, 2024). Such benefits are also a great recruiting tool for prospective employees that are local to the organization or dispersed around the world.

Organizations should offer comprehensive health and wellness benefits that support employees' physical, mental, and emotional well-being (Androniceanu, Kinnunen, Georgescu & Androniceanu, 2020). Many examples of such benefits are offered by innovative organizations as a means of helping their employees establish and maintain their health and the health of their respective families.

Many employers of health insurance plans that cover preventive care, mental health services, and wellness programs may subsidize them to offset some of the cost so employees can get insured at a much lower cost than pursuing coverage individually.

In addition to the health insurance, employers may offer Employee assistance programs (EAPs) that provide confidential counseling and support services. Sometimes the organizations may employ EAP Counselors that are dedicated to providing direct assistance to the employees. Other organizations contract out the EAP services to a private EAP organization who provides the same services. In either case, the employees and their respective family members are afforded great care to ensure they can perform their work roles at their peak.

In today's work environment, it is difficult to find organizations that do not provide on-site or subsidized fitness facilities, classes, or memberships. Employees are more health oriented and look for these benefits in jobs they decide to take on. Innovative organizations usually lead the way in meeting employees desire to have access to a gym at or near their work location.

Healthy food options and snacks in the workplace have become a relatively new but expanding trend, especially with technology-based companies. In these organizations, employees are able to get free food and snacks during the workday, so they never have to leave work to satisfy their thirst or hunger. While it seems to be a huge expense for the employer, it may work in the employer's favor because employees eat and work at the same time and productivity levels may only decrease slightly as compared to the when the employees leave work to get food and drinks. Investing in employee health and wellness, organizations can reduce healthcare costs, improve productivity and engagement, and demonstrate their commitment to employee well-being.

In today's always-on, hyper-connected work environment, it's important for organizations to encourage employees to take time off and disconnect from work.

Organizations can consider a range of remedies to assist employees in maintaining a healthy work-life balance by instituting mandatory vacation policies or unlimited paid time off to get people to take a break from work and recharge. For those people that really have a hard time letting go of their work and continually check work messages when they should be on the golf course, the organization may need to create "No email" policies outside of work hours or on weekends. In general, organizations may already offer vacation and sick leave to employees, so they are not obligated to show up at work when they are not at their best. In addition, organization-wide "recharge days" or mental health days may be offered to ensure that employees get needed time away from the job to enjoy life. It is essentially important to encourage leaders to model healthy work-life boundaries and take time off themselves, as well. Promoting a culture of rest and renewal increases the chances that organizations can help employees avoid burnout, recharge their creativity, and bring fresh perspectives to their work. Margaret Heffernan suggests in her book "Beyond Measure" that people must allow their brains to wonder. Walking outside does wonders to allow people to recharge by disengaging from work tasks and allowing down time to enjoy nature and exercise before returning to the office (Heffernan, 2015).

A supportive and inclusive workplace culture is essential for employee well-being and engagement. Organizations can foster this type of culture by promoting open and transparent communication and feedback and by providing opportunities for social connection and team building.

Celebrating diversity and inclusion and addressing any instances of discrimination or harassment are critical to establishing and maintaining a stable work environment that is welcoming to everyone. Offering mentoring, coaching, and professional development opportunities is a great way to have employees and leadership to build healthy and nurturing relationships that helps people build competence and confidence with peers and leaders within the work environment. Creating a workplace culture that values and supports employees as whole people can improve retention, motivation, and innovation (DiJulius, and Murray, 2024).

Many employees today are also caregivers for children, aging parents, or other family members. Organizations can support these employees by offering backup childcare or eldercare services and by providing flexible leave policies for caregiving responsibilities. Organizations can assist employees by connecting employees with community resources and support groups. In addition, offering seminars or workshops on caregiving topics, such as aging parents or special needs children is a great way to provide the support that employees need to take their minds off external concerns. Acknowledging and supporting the caregiving responsibilities of their employees, organizations can reduce stress and absenteeism and improve job satisfaction and loyalty (DiJulius, and Murray, 2024). After the COVID-19 pandemic, employers realized that their people could work remotely and still be incredibly productive. This also allows them to provide the care to family members in their respective homes without missing a beat when it comes to work productivity. Many jobs are task oriented and do not require meetings. These tasks may be performed off-camera and at odd hours of the day. Organizations should understand remote, and hybrid work is imperative for younger generation employees (e.g. Gen-Z) thrive in an environment that allows for flexible working styles. Employers that recognize these opportunities can save money on office space and still get the productivity from employees as they take care of their family and work requirements, respectively.

Finally, organizations should regularly measure and address employee well-being and work-life balance. Organizations can create and conduct employee surveys and focus groups on stress, burnout, and work-life conflict. Organizations can gain key insights on problem areas by analyzing data on absenteeism, turnover, and healthcare costs related to stress and burnout. Additionally, audits of workload and job demands may be performed to help identify areas for improvement. Using such techniques, the organization may perform comparative analysis to benchmark against industry best practices and innovative companies who may be competitors. Continuously improving and adapting policies and programs based on employee feedback and needs can uncover needed adjustments to remain viable and perhaps outpace competitors.

By proactively measuring and addressing employee well-being and work-life balance, organizations can create a more sustainable and human-centered approach to innovation and success. Supporting employee well-being and work-life balance requires a multi-faceted approach that includes flexible work arrangements, comprehensive health and wellness benefits, encouragement of time off and disconnection, a supportive and inclusive workplace culture, resources for caregivers, and ongoing measurement and improvement. Prioritizing employee well-being is a key driver of innovation success.

PART IV

Driving Innovation through Organizational Structures

CHAPTER 17

Optimizing Structures for Innovation

"The secret of change is to focus all of your energy not on fighting the old, but on building the new."

—Socrates

When it comes to driving innovation, organizational structures play a crucial role in facilitating or hindering the process. Traditional hierarchical structures with rigid departmental silos and top-down decision-making can often stifle creativity, collaboration, and agility. To foster a culture of innovation, organizations need to evaluate and optimize their structures to promote flexibility, cross-functional collaboration, and rapid experimentation (Kamasak, 2015). There are important considerations for evaluating and optimizing organizational structures for innovation.

Organizational leaders must assess current structures and communication constructs and their impact on innovation. They can start by conducting a thorough assessment of the organization's current structures and their impact on innovation. In an innovative organization, the leadership and the workforce must have open lines of communication to make sure that everyone is on the same page. Employees must understand how they communicate their ideas to leadership such that decisions may be made about acceptance or rejection of the idea as a potential innovation. Mapping out the formal and informal lines of communication and decision-making processes is critical for everyone in the organization to understand (Kamasak, 2015). Identifying silos or barriers to collaboration and information sharing must be addressed so strengthen the organizational knowledge. When in competition with other organizations, speed is of the utmost importance so communications and decision-making processes must be responsive in both directions because the viability of a potential innovation may be lost due to latency, therefore, analyzing the speed and agility of decision-making and resource allocation processes is a critical step that must be taken into account when attempting to increase the organization's agility.

In addition to becoming more responsive in communications, decision-making and resource allocation, teams and individuals must be given decision authority within their own domains. So, assessing the level of autonomy and empowerment of teams and individuals and determining thresholds for leadership decisions and those decisions relegated to teams and individuals must be established and understood at all levels of the organization. Gathering feedback from employees on how current structures support or hinder their ability to innovate is a great place to begin this exercise, because all perspectives would be considered and implemented in ways that incorporate the values and concerns of all levels of the organization. Based on this assessment, identify areas for improvement and prioritize changes that will have the greatest impact on innovation.

One of the most effective ways to promote innovation is to flatten hierarchies and decentralize decision-making (Jantz, 2012). While this seems like a drastic move, there are ways to gain the benefit of innovation without a complete organizational makeover. Just as was mentioned in the previous section, by allocating decision authorities at different levels within the organization, some synergy may be achieved. The idea is to improve communications and business processes in ways that create the internal agility necessary to keep pace or surpass competitors.

Reducing layers of management and bureaucracy can greatly improve the effectiveness of operations. In a typical hierarchical organization, decision authority for a great number of business functions occurs at a very high level. Cutting out unnecessary approvals enables processes to be streamlined to deliver outcomes at the speed of business (Jantz, 2012). Empowering teams and individuals to make decisions benefits directly from the streamlined processes and it allows them more control and accountability for their work.

When organizational leaders provide clear goals and guardrails, but allow for flexibility and experimentation within those parameters, it inculcates a culture of trust, transparency, and accountability within the workforce at all levels. It also conditions leaders to act more in the capacity of coaches and facilitators, rather than controllers decision-makers. Flattening hierarchies and decentralizing decision-making, organizations create a more agile and responsive environment that enables innovation to flourish.

A staple in modern business is the hierarchy that defines the leadership from the management and the management from the workers. It also defines how communication from the top of the hierarchy to all the lower levels. The hierarchical structure resembles the shape of a pyramid that depicts the distribution of people within the organization (Jantz, 2012). There are a few people at the top who provide the vision and the leadership to the organization. The middle of the hierarchy depicts the management level who are organized to provide oversight of their respective portfolios and the people at the lowest level of the hierarchy who perform the nuts and bolts work of the organization. This traditional corporate organizational structure is referred to as a Top-Down structure.

As innovation goes within an organization, the leaders must pave the way for the innovators. In a sense, this move causes the organizational leaders to switch places with the people pursuing innovations. The innovators and their supporting cast will make demands of the organization such as resources and access to information that is not routinely available outside of the innovation process.

So now, the organizational leadership works for the innovators. The professional status of the innovators is irrelevant in the process. When they need assistance or resources, the organizational leaders are obligated to engage and provide the requested help.

Top-Down leadership indicates that the vision and corporate behavior emanates from the top of the organization and flows down to the lower levels (Jantz, 2012). Corporate policies and strategic goals are set at this level and determine the products and services that the organization will focus on for some defined period of time. People at the top tier of the hierarchical pyramid have titles that begin with the letter 'C', such as Chief Executive Officer (CEO), Chief Operating Officer (COO), Chief Information Officer (CIO), Chief Information Security Officer (CISO), Chief Human Capital Officer (CHCO) and Chief Innovation Officer (CINO). These corporate officers collectively form something called the Board of Directors and each is accountable for their respective corporate portfolios. Each corporate officer exercises span of control for their respective portfolios and collectively the Board of Directors are responsible for the fate of the entire organization.

The Chief Innovation Officer (CINO) is a C-suite executive level position with organization-wide responsibility for innovation strategy and execution. The CINO sets the overall enterprise innovation strategy aligned with business objectives. To ensure the CINO can enforce the innovation strategy, they customarily oversee the corporate innovation budget and associated resource allocation. The CINO is accountable for fostering an innovation culture across the entire organization and they also represent innovation interests at the highest level of decision-making. That accountability extends to achieving corporate innovation outcomes

Each of the corporate officer roles are governed by rigid rules and principles that protect and enable the organization to perform its work ethically and legally while ensuring the organization is satisfying the organization's strategic goals. All the behaviors of the management and works are determined by the manner in which the organization decides to deliver value to its customers. The corporate leaders are typically people who possess a wealth of knowledge to best guide the organization. Typically, the people serving in these corporate leadership roles hold their positions for long periods of time, which provides corporate stability. The organizational culture grows out of the corporate structure, the rules it puts into place for its people, the level of corporate risk it is willing to accept and the incentive practices.

Within the organizational hierarchy, the workforce is commoditized and represents the most volatile in terms of career mobility. People come into and exit the workforce on a continual basis. This reality means that new people are oriented to the organization and are absorbed into the culture and taught the value system and knowledge to perform the work they were hired to do. The people that exit the workforce, however, carry with them a portion of the organization's intellectual property and ideas they had to improve the bottom line of the organization. They did not have an opportunity or were discouraged from taking risks to yield a better outcome for the organization because the ideas may have been perceived as too risky. In a heavily controlled and rigid environment, the opportunity to innovate is diminished or even discouraged because the organization has determined the way in which business will be conducted by everyone employed by the organization. This means that innovation opportunities in such environments are limited.

There are too many examples of traditionally organized corporate entities that have failed to thrive because they fail to innovate. With a top-down approach the most precious resource available to the organization is wasted, its people. The belief that all facets of the organization must be rigidly controlled to be successful is the act that drives the organization to oblivion. Everyone possesses talents and when challenged to get a job done using their individual talents, magic happens. If leadership wants to tap into the intellectual gold mine that resides within the organization's workforce, then the organization must learn to run flat!

Each year, surveys are published citing the best companies to work for from the perspective of the employees. A trait at the center of positive ratings is corporate culture. The corporate workforce is invited to contribute their respective talents to help the company thrive. All employee-contribution ideas are given consideration and possibly pursued as a means to help the organization's bottom line. Employees feel a sense of pride in helping the company achieve its goals.

While running flat sounds like a monumental undertaking, it can be made simple to understand and to implement. The establishment of specific norms and processes are essential in transforming into a flat organization. One such norm is that the corporate leadership must respect the ideas and talents of their employees. The corporate leadership must encourage, listen to and act on ideas contributed by employees. This may be implementing processes the organization invites its personnel to participate in. Organizations may remain hierarchical and take on the characteristics of flat organizations. Leaders and employees maintain their respective status, but running flat means that behaviors are transformed.

Corporate leadership meetings are scheduled on a recurring basis such that leaders can plan and organize to meet the corporate goals. In such meetings the general direction of the company is discussed, and the leaders contribute their respective ideas. Ideas are contributed, evaluated, and acted upon. Afterwards, corporate guidance is given, and the workforce acts accordingly. This scenario is typical of most corporations. It is a top-down decision run organization that treats employees as tools. In a flat model, equal value must be placed on engaging the employees. A recurring meeting time in a designated place must be established such that corporate leadership can establish a meaningful relationship that benefits the bottom line of the company.

A typical decision process involves the employee contributing an idea to their first line management. The manager then submits the idea to the next level up in the leadership hierarchy until it reaches a leader with decision authority. Once the decision is made, the approval is passed back down to the hierarchy for implementation. The approval process is not depicted in its fullness, however. As the process advances, so does time. Inefficient decision management for proposed ideas unnecessarily weakens the intended outcomes the ideas were intended to generate.

In a flat organization corporate leadership is available to the employees. The employees and the leadership converse freely and everyone feel like a part of the organization. Employees contribute their ideas and apply their unique talents to aid the company in delivering the best possible products and services. The turnaround time is shortened because ideas are offered, considered, and implemented (or not). The process is consistent, open to all and directly impactful to the company's bottom line.

While most companies would not reorganize from a hierarchical to a flat model, there is a means of reaping the described benefits. The benefits are best captured by the behavior of the organization and not its hard structure. For instance, leadership making themselves available to engage employees and their respective ideas can be satisfied with recurring meetings. Employees can plan between such meetings about the ideas they wish to present to management because all the meeting dates are programmed into the calendar.

To the leadership, this is one more meeting to attend that is focused on bettering the company. To the employees, this represents an opportunity to challenge the company and its employees by asking it to consider ideas that were not pre-planned but have outstanding potential benefits.

In any reasonable innovation process, time is a major consideration for testing ideas as potential solutions to pressing business challenges. Any means of shortening the timeline for gaining approval to consider an idea for experimentation is going to put the organization in a better position in their chosen business domain. Organizing periodic presentations of ideas to a group of investors allows the organization leaders to learn how to use the entire set of faculties to advance the organization's position in the business domain. The corporate leadership and management gain a better understanding of the risks and challenges, and the innovators get to demonstrate their knowledge and concerns through the expression of offered ideas to solve problems that everyone will agree need to be solved. Corporate leaders in this engagement should scrutinize the proposed ideas under consideration but must be careful not to say no to everything that gets presented.

Innovation often happens at the intersections of different disciplines, perspectives, and experiences. To facilitate this type of cross-pollination, organizations should create structures that promote cross-functional collaboration and networking. Fusing organizational knowledge can be best facilitated by forming dedicated innovation teams or labs that bring together diverse talent from across the organization. A routine practice in hierarchical organizations is the creation of project-based or matrix structures that allow employees to work on multiple initiatives and collaborate with different teams.

In addition to the cross-function team construct, encouraging the formation of communities of practice or interest groups

141

around specific topics or challenges can also be very effective from the innovation perspective.

Given the organization is committed to building out its innovation ecosystem. providing physical and virtual spaces for employees to connect, share ideas, and work together will be a central concern. This is true for the employees who are physically located at the organization's facilities or those employees who work remotely or deployed with different time zones. If committed to breaking down silos and creating structures that enable cross-functional collaboration, organizations can tap into the full potential of their diverse talent and expertise.

Adaptable innovation methodologies offer several key characteristics and benefits that make them well-suited for organizations looking to foster creativity and drive successful innovation. Some of the main characteristics of Adaptable Innovation Methodologies include but are not limited to the following:

✦ **Modularity:** Adaptable methodologies are composed of modular elements that can be mixed, matched, and rearranged to fit the specific needs and preferences of the organization. This allows for customization and tailoring of the innovation process.

✦ **Iterative nature:** These methodologies emphasize iterative cycles of ideation, prototyping, testing, and refinement. This enables continuous improvement and the ability to pivot based on feedback and new insights.

✦ **Collaboration-focused:** Adaptable methodologies prioritize cross-functional collaboration and the inclusion of diverse perspectives. They encourage open communication, knowledge sharing, and co-creation among team members.

✦ **Context-sensitive:** These approaches take into account the unique context of the organization, including its culture, resources, and strategic goals. They can be adapted to align with the company's existing processes and practices.

There are great benefits of adaptable innovation methodologies because they can grow along with the needs of the organization. The adaptable nature of these methodologies allows organizations to respond quickly to changing market conditions, customer needs, and technological advancements. They enable agility and the ability to seize new opportunities as they arise. Additionally, fostering collaboration and encouraging diverse perspectives, adaptable methodologies create an environment conducive to creative problem-solving. This can lead to more innovative ideas and solutions.

The modular and iterative aspects of adaptable methodologies help streamline the innovation process, reducing waste and minimizing the risk of investing in unviable ideas. The ability to test and refine concepts early on saves time and resources. When team members have the flexibility to shape the innovation process according to their preferences and expertise, they are more likely to feel a sense of ownership and engagement. This can lead to higher motivation and commitment to the project's success. Adaptable methodologies can be tailored to support the organization's strategic objectives and key performance indicators. This ensures that innovation efforts are focused on areas that will deliver the most value to the company. These approaches provide frameworks and principles that can be customized and adapted to suit the specific needs of the organization.

Adaptable innovation methodologies offer a flexible and dynamic approach to driving innovation within organizations.

Embracing modularity, iteration, collaboration, and context-sensitivity, these methodologies enable companies to foster creativity, improve efficiency, and align their innovation efforts with strategic goals. As organizations navigate an increasingly complex and rapidly changing business landscape, the ability to adapt and innovate becomes a critical competitive advantage.

Organizations can implement adaptable innovation methodologies through a combination of strategic planning, cultural shifts, and practical measures. There are ways to effectively integrate these methodologies into an organization's innovation environment. Organizations must consider their existing innovation practices, identifying strengths, weaknesses, and areas for improvement. This assessment will help determine which aspects of adaptable methodologies would be most beneficial to implement. The organization must also invest in training programs that educate employees about the principles, tools, and techniques of adaptable innovation methodologies. This will help build a shared understanding and foster a culture of innovation throughout the organization.

Create diverse, cross-functional teams that bring together individuals with different backgrounds, skills, and perspectives. This collaborative approach facilitates the sharing of ideas and encourages creative problem-solving. Promote a culture that values experimentation, learning from failure, and continuous improvement. Encourage teams to prototype ideas quickly, gather feedback, and iterate based on the insights gained.

One of the possibilities of adaptation should be the incorporation of existing processes used within the organization. Examine the organization's current processes and identify opportunities to integrate adaptable innovation methodologies. For example, incorporating Design Thinking principles into product development or applying Agile practices to project management. Create platforms and events that facilitate the exchange of ideas, best practices, and lessons learned. Regularly evaluate the effectiveness of the implemented adaptable innovation methodologies. Seek feedback from employees, customers, and stakeholders to identify areas for improvement and make necessary adjustments.

Some specific examples of how organizations have successfully implemented adaptable innovation methodologies include:

✦ **Procter & Gamble's "Connect + Develop"** program, which leverages external partnerships and open innovation to drive new product development (Ozkan, 2015).

✦ **IBM's "Design Thinking"** approach, which has been integrated into various aspects of the company's operations, from product design to customer experience (IBM, 2016).

✦ **Intuit's "Design for Delight"** methodology, which resembles a modified Design Thinking approach that combines customer empathy, rapid experimentation, and continuous iteration to create innovative financial products and services (Intuit, 2019).

Implementing adaptable innovation methodologies requires a commitment to organizational change, a willingness to embrace new ways of working, and a focus on continuous learning and improvement. Using a strategic and holistic approach, organizations can harness the power of these methodologies to drive innovation, stay competitive, and create value for their customers and stakeholders. Embracing adaptable methodologies, organizations can create structures that enable faster time-to-market, higher quality solutions, and more responsive innovation.

To ensure that innovation remains a strategic priority and receives the necessary resources and support, organizations may need to establish dedicated innovation roles and functions (Alves, Galina, 2018). These could include:

✦ **Chief Innovation Officers** who are responsible for setting the innovation strategy and driving alignment across the organization

✦ **Innovation coaches** who provide training, facilitation, and support to teams and individual innovators

✦ **Innovation researchers** who identify emerging trends, technologies, and opportunities

✦ **Innovation ambassadors** who promote and model innovation behaviors and mindsets

✦ **Innovation councils** that provide governance and oversight for company level innovation initiatives

The roles and their descriptions are examples only. Organizations must create roles that reflect their innovation goals and attach the appropriate responsibility and accountability to the named roles. Establishing dedicated innovation roles and functions, organizations can create the structures and capabilities needed to sustain and scale innovation over time.

Finally, organizations should continuously evaluate and adapt their structures for innovation based on changing business needs, market conditions, and employee feedback. To this end, they must regularly assess the effectiveness and efficiency of current structures and processes and look to improve them where appropriate. They should experiment with new structures, roles, or methodologies to drive innovation and adapt their processes and overall methodology where appropriate. Everything that happens with innovation does not have to be discovered locally. The organization should seek out best practices and lessons learned from other innovative organizations. The provisioning of innovation scaffolding should not be done solely by high-level organizational leaders. It should be done instead by engaging employees in the design and improvement of innovation-friendly structures (Esposito, 2023). Any resulting changes or adaptations to the methodology or its underlying processes must be communicated and celebrated especially when the impact of structural positively affects innovation outcomes. Adopting a continuous improvement mindset and being willing to adapt and evolve their structures over time, organizations can create a more resilient and future-proof approach to innovation.

In summary, evaluating and optimizing organizational structures for innovation requires a multi-faceted approach that includes assessing current structures, flattening hierarchies, creating cross-functional teams and networks, implementing adaptable methodologies, establishing dedicated innovation roles and functions, and continuously adapting and improving structures over time (Alves, Galina, 2018). Designing structures that enable flexibility, collaboration, experimentation, and learning, organizations can create the conditions for sustainable and impactful innovation (Esposito, 2023).

CHAPTER 18

Corporate Innovation Oversight

"Innovation happens at the intersection of freedom and structure."

—Tim Brown

B alancing centralized and decentralized decision-making is a critical consideration when it comes to innovation governance (Wale, 2024). Centralized decision-making can provide strategic alignment, consistency, and efficiency, while decentralized decision-making can enable autonomy, adaptability, and responsiveness at the local level. The key is to find the right balance that enables both strategic coherence and operational flexibility. Balancing centralized and decentralized decision-making in innovation governance helps to provide clarity of responsibility and accountability at various levels within the organization (Nooraie, 2014).

The corporate or executive level should be responsible for setting the overall innovation strategy, priorities, and goals for the organization. To make certain that everyone in the workforce at all levels is clear on the innovation vision and mission, it must be clearly and unambiguously defined and conveyed by the organizational leadership. Leaders must make certain that innovation is not a passing fad but a way to do business going forward. As the vision and mission of innovation within the organization are laid out, there must be clear ties to the strategic goals of the organization, so members of the workforce understanding that innovation is the means by which the organization will achieve success.

To accomplish the strategic goals of the organization, leaders must identify the key strategic areas or domains where innovation activities must be emphasized. While such guidance is instructive to the workforce, it is rather broad and allows for a range of activities to occur in each of the identified emphasis categories.

The focus on innovation is key to the organization's future and it must overcome the inefficiencies of the traditional methods to produce quality products and services at a faster rate. To this end, leaders must set performance metrics and targets for innovation and track the progress over time and in comparison, to traditional (or non-innovative) outcomes.

To achieve the full potential of innovation within the organization, leaders must commit to allocating resources and budgets to bolster innovation initiatives (Nooraie, 2014). Such leadership support sends the positive message to the workforce that innovation is valued by the organization and their participation in these activities is expected. When transforming an organization from a traditional footing to an innovative footing, communicating

the innovation strategy and priorities to the entire organization must be a repetitive act. When leaders provide clear strategic direction and priorities at the corporate level and throughout the workforce the organization can ensure that innovation efforts are aligned with the overall business strategy and values.

While the corporate level sets the overall strategy and priorities, teams and individuals should be empowered to make decisions and take actions within a strategic framework (Nooraie, 2014). To help this process along, leadership must provide clear guidelines and criteria for innovation projects and investments. To lower the burden on the organizational leadership while giving responsibilities to others within the workforce, some of the decision-making authority should be delegated to the lowest possible level, based on expertise and context (Wale, 2024). Employees must be encouraged to engage in experimentation and calculated risk-taking within defined parameters. To facilitate the experimentation, the organization must provide the tools, resources, and support for local decision-making and problem-solving.

Teams and individuals are likely to feel better about their work when given the latitude to make decisions that directly impact work being conducted at their respective levels within the organization. This fosters a culture of trust, accountability, and continuous learning and these factors are essential in building and growing a culture of innovation. Empowering teams and individuals to make decisions within strategic guardrails, organizations can enable faster, more contextual innovation and build a sense of ownership and engagement at all levels.

To ensure that innovation efforts are aligned, coordinated, and accountable, organizations need to establish clear governance structures and processes. This implies that the organization has the means of communicating to the entire workforce to get everyone on the same page concerning existing and planned innovation activities. While organizational communications are vital to this process, so is the establishment of tangible constructs that model the contents of the communications. Employees need to relate the communications by engaging the innovation methodology, the practices, processes and people to reinforce the corporate messaging.

Defining roles and responsibilities for innovation decision-making at different levels (e.g., corporate, business unit, project team) is an important step in matching the words to the actions. The creation of well-defined innovation roles helps to inculcate innovation concepts and practices within all facets of the business. With these roles in place employees can approach the people serving in those roles to get insights, guidance and mentoring when considering ideas, they believe would be wonderful innovations for the organization.

To further enforce organizational alignment of innovation to strategic goals, the establishment of innovation councils, committees, or boards may be created to provide oversight and guidance across all organizational innovation activities. A concern in this approach, however, may send message to the workforce that the hierarchy is still in effect. Ideally, these organizational constructs, if implemented, should be lightweight to avoid becoming another layer of organizational bureaucracy (Schneeweiss, 2010).

In the earlier discussions concerning experimentation and the establishment of physical and virtual spaces in which innovation activities would be conducted, the organization must present a tangible representation of the innovation methodology's process so that employees gain an appreciation for how to transform ideas into potential innovations. Creating stage-gate or portfolio management processes for evaluating and prioritizing innovation projects is one way to accomplish that goal. Such a process should be fully explained to the workforce and have well-understood explanations that cover all issues from idea submission to final realization of an innovations resulting from submitted ideas. Implementing metrics and reporting systems to track innovation performance and outcomes is also an important consideration that must be explained to the workforce and made available to leadership for impact assessment of innovation efforts in the organization. While innovation efforts are producing value for the organization, this information must be shared with the workforce on a continuous basis to keep them in the loop and interested in innovation. Establishing communications channels, effort feedback and mechanisms for continuous improvement and learning are all necessary facets of successful innovation within an organization. Putting in place clear governance structures and processes, organizations can strike a balance between centralized control and decentralized autonomy and ensure that innovation efforts are aligned with strategic priorities and delivering value.

Innovation often requires collaboration and knowledge sharing across different functions, business units, and geographies (Jia and Xia, 2008). To enable this type of collaboration, organizations should create cross-functional innovation teams or networks. Studies have shown that diversity of ideas is essential in producing the best possible innovation outcomes. That diversity of ideas stems from the diversity of people selected to compose the various teams.

While each team may become optimized within their own innovation efforts, insights gained from those activities should be shared widely within the organization to educate others about the knowledge gained as well as issues that hindered progress. The organization should consider establishing knowledge-sharing platforms and communities of practice to expand opportunities to share valuable insights to audiences outside of the local sphere of innovation activities. This can be performed with commercial tooling or application-specific tooling that may be built and used in-house. Such implementation encourages open communication and dialogue across silos and levels within the organization. To spur increased engagement from the workforce, the organization should provide incentives and recognition for collaboration and knowledge sharing. This helps to foster a culture of diversity and inclusion that could result in higher employee participation and higher impact from resulting innovations. Promoting cross-functional teaming, collaboration and knowledge sharing, organizations can break down silos, leverage diverse perspectives and expertise, and enable more holistic and impactful innovation (Jia and Xia, 2008).

The optimal balance of centralized and decentralized decision-making may vary depending on the organization's size, industry, culture, and stage of innovation maturity. Therefore, it's important to continuously evaluate and adjust the balance. As the organization's workforce dynamics change over time, the organization's requirements to support locally based employees and distributed employees changes, as well. This is particularly true when discussing the impact of the organization's innovation efforts. As discussed earlier, access to key personnel to get guidance and mentoring for employees who operate in different time zones may be problematic when those key personnel have non-overlapping work hours. This concern could be addressed with the use of asynchronous communications and the implementation of virtualized AI entities to provide assistance to innovators within different time zones.

The organization can get feedback and input from teams and individuals involved in innovation, both locally and in differing geographic locations. When the organization wishes to assess the impact of innovation, it must take into account efforts across all locations by conducting an analysis of innovation performance metrics and outcomes. The data from the analysis should be benchmarked against industry best practices and peer organizations. Such activities should take into consideration the changes in the external market, technological, or regulatory environment. It should also take into account the evolution of the organization's strategy, structure, or capabilities over time (Schneeweiss, 2010). Adopting a flexible and adaptive approach to innovation governance, organizations can find the right balance of centralization and decentralization for their specific context and goals (Nooraie, 2014).

Balancing centralized and decentralized decision-making in innovation governance requires defining clear strategies and priorities at the corporate level, empowering teams and individuals within strategic guardrails, establishing clear governance structures and processes, fostering cross-functional collaboration and knowledge sharing, and continuously evaluating and adjusting the balance based on feedback and performance (Schneeweiss, 2010). Striking the right balance for organizations can ensure both strategic alignment and operational agility and create the conditions for impactful innovation.

CHAPTER 19

Creating Dedicated Innovation Teams and Roles

"Innovation is not about saying yes to everything. It's about saying NO to all but the most crucial features."

—Steve Jobs

Creating dedicated innovation teams and roles can be a powerful way to drive innovation in organizations, but it also comes with potential drawbacks and challenges. Some of the features and faults of this approach are explored here. Dedicated innovation teams bring together individuals with diverse skills and backgrounds who are solely focused on innovation that benefits the organization. This allows them to develop deep expertise in innovation processes, tools, and methodologies, and apply them consistently across the organization. While this is mostly true for teams that are located within the same geographical setting, it can be a challenge for members of the organization who are deployed in different time zones and do not have ready access to experts to guide and mentor them, accordingly. As discussed previously, innovation teams should be composed of members of the workforce who serve as experts in specific roles and help fellow innovators apply their respective knowledge and skill, in context, throughout their respective innovation pursuits.

Ideally, the deployed innovators should receive consistent experiences when engaging innovation coaches, mentors and technical experts. Due to the reality that people serving in the named roles are the product of unique knowledge, skill and innovation background, such consistency cannot be assured. Virtualized AI-based avatars created to serve is these capacities, however, may be a potential means of addressing the issue, but care must be given to ensure that the deployed innovator gains the same benefits as innovators who are local to the organization's main physical facilities.

Creating dedicated teams that are not bogged down by day-to-day operations and bureaucracy can accelerate the pace of innovation and respond more quickly to emerging opportunities or threats. When engaged in an innovation pursuit. The innovation team must be composed of volunteers from within the organization who serve for a defined length of time in their respective roles and then return back to their internal home organizations. This ensures that the volunteer's leadership is bought into the innovation culture by allowing them employees to participate in the larger organization's innovation activity (Fouejieu, 2023). Secondly, the agility is created when each of the roles are vacated and filled with entirely new people. The new people perform in the same roles, but their professional and cultural experiences are different than those of their immediate predecessors. This means that the advice, mentorship and coaching they provide to the innovators may be vastly different.

A staple in the innovation world is continuous collaboration and knowledge sharing. Innovation teams are often cross-functional, bringing together individuals from different departments and disciplines. This diversity of perspectives can lead to more creative and holistic solutions and help break down silos and foster collaboration across the organization (Morehead, 2022). It also enhances the exchange of critical information through casual conversations about the innovation efforts and also formally through the documentation that is generated within the innovative processes (Fouejieu, 2023). With a dedicated team and budget, organizations can more easily track and measure the impact of innovation efforts and demonstrate the value and ROI of innovation to stakeholders.

Dedicated innovation teams are often given the freedom and resources to experiment with new ideas and take calculated risks. This can create a culture of innovation and entrepreneurship and generate new growth opportunities for the organization. In general, having the latitude to control the fate of innovation efforts locally indicates a level of trust that the organizational leaders have given to the lower-level teams. This move demonstrates the level of trust and confidence that organizational leaders have in the team's ability to diligently explore the innovation effort and also police themselves to stay within the strategic goal framework while doing so.

Just as the features were highlighted, there are some downsides to the issues of constructing innovation teams and enabling them to operate without the benefit of routine corporate oversight. Some of those concerns are identified along their potential to produce outcomes that are not strategically aligned with corporate goals. If innovation teams are too separate from the rest of the organization, they may become isolated and disconnected from the day-to-day realities and needs of the business. This can lead to innovations that are not practical, relevant, or aligned with the overall strategy. Clear and constant communication with leadership, stakeholders and customers is required to ensure that innovation pursuits are aligned with the organization's vision and meets the needs of the customer and expectations of the stakeholders. Such communication may be initiated by the team or any of the interested parties.

Dedicated innovation teams can sometimes be seen as a threat or distraction by other parts of the organization, leading to resistance, lack of buy-in, or even sabotage of innovation efforts. This can be particularly challenging if the innovation team is seen as receiving special treatment or resources. Innovations developed by dedicated teams may be difficult to scale and integrate into the broader organization, particularly if they require significant changes to processes, systems, or culture. This can lead to innovations that are not fully leveraged or that fail to deliver their full potential value. If the function of innovation is seen as the sole responsibility of a dedicated team, other parts of the organization may become overly dependent on them and lack accountability for driving innovation in their own areas. This can create a culture of complacency and limit the overall innovation capacity of the organization.

Building and maintaining a dedicated innovation team requires significant investments in talent, resources, and infrastructure. This can be challenging for organizations with limited budgets or competing priorities and may not be sustainable over the long term. In fact, one of the biggest points of contention in traditional organizations is the tight control on local resources. This includes the local organization's people who may be assigned to projects of significant importance to the larger organization's strategic goals. Acquiring the time and focus of selected employees to populate the innovation team could introduce risk to the success of the local projects to which they are assigned. The anticipated potential impact of the envisioned innovation, however, may drive the ultimate decision.

While dedicated teams can be a catalyst for innovation, it's important to foster a culture of innovation and entrepreneurship across the entire organization and empower all employees to contribute ideas and drive change. Organizations can further enhance the production of the team by offering training to help employees across the organization develop innovation skills and capabilities and provide resources and tools to enable them to participate in innovation efforts. There is also great value in celebrating the successes of innovation teams and sharing them widely across the organization, while also providing support and resources to help scale and integrate promising innovations into the broader business.

Regularly assess the effectiveness and impact of dedicated innovation teams and be willing to adapt the model as needed based on feedback, performance, and changing business needs.

Creating dedicated innovation teams and roles can be a powerful way to accelerate and focus innovation efforts, but it also comes with potential challenges and drawbacks. Ensuring strategic alignment, fostering a culture of innovation across the organization, providing training and support, celebrating and scaling successes, and continuously adapting the model leverages the benefits of dedicated innovation teams while mitigating the potential faults (Grivas, 2011).

CHAPTER 20

Fostering Internal Entrepreneurship and Intrapreneurship

"The enterprise that does not innovate ages and declines. And in a period of rapid change such as the present, the decline will be fast."

—Peter Drucker

Fostering internal entrepreneurship and intrapreneurship is a key strategy for driving innovation and growth within established organizations. Intrapreneurship refers to the practice of encouraging and supporting employees to think and act like entrepreneurs within the context of their existing organization (Wiener, 2023). Fostering a culture of intrapreneurship helps to tap into the creativity, passion, and expertise of their employees, and create new opportunities for innovation and value creation.

Employees may be given the freedom and autonomy to identify and pursue new ideas and opportunities within their areas of expertise. They should be encouraged to take ownership of their projects and decisions and provide them with the resources and support they need to bring their ideas to fruition. It is important for organizations to offer training and development programs that help employees develop entrepreneurial skills and mindsets, such as creativity, problem-solving, critical thinking, and calculated risk-taking. Provide opportunities for employees to learn about new technologies, business models, and industry trends that could inspire new ideas and innovations.

Organizational leaders must help to foster a culture that values experimentation, iteration, and learning from failure. Encourage employees to test and validate their ideas through small-scale pilots, prototypes, or minimum viable products, and provide them with the resources and support they need to iterate and improve based on feedback and data.

Clear processes and criteria must be established for evaluating, prioritizing, and funding internal innovation projects. These processes must ensure transparency, objectivity, and alignment with the overall strategy and goals of the organization. They should provide guidance and support to help employees navigate these processes and make a compelling case for their ideas.

These corporate entities must recognize and celebrate employees who demonstrate entrepreneurial thinking and behaviors, and who create value for the organization through their innovations. Organizations must provide both financial and non-financial incentives, such as bonuses, equity, promotions, or public recognition, to encourage and reward intrapreneurship at all levels of the organization (Nimergood, 2014).

Collaboration and knowledge sharing across different functions are essential across all levels of the organization. Opportunities must be offered to employees to work on cross-functional teams, participate in hackathons or innovation challenges, or engage in peer mentoring and coaching. This can help break down silos, spark new ideas, and create a more cohesive and supportive culture of intrapreneurship.

Employees must be provided with adequate resources and networks they need to develop and scale their ideas, such as funding, technology, market research, customer insights, or external partnerships. Establishment of internal innovation funds or accelerators goes a long way to provide seed funding and support for promising intrapreneurial projects, and connect employees with relevant experts, mentors, or advisors who can provide guidance and feedback.

Corporate leaders and managers can team to ensure that intrapreneurial initiatives are aligned with the overall strategy, values, and priorities of the organization. These priorities should be routinely communicated across the enterprise as clearly and consistently as possible to help employees understand how their ideas and innovations contribute to the bigger picture (Gunaratne, 2001). Regular updates and feedback must be given on the progress and impact of intrapreneurial projects and seek input and involvement from key stakeholders across the organization.

Organizations must strike a balance between providing structure and processes to guide and support intrapreneurship and allowing for flexibility and adaptability as ideas evolve and circumstances change. Corporate leaders must be willing to adjust timelines, resources, or expectations based on feedback and learning, and empower employees to pivot or persevere as needed to achieve their goals.

Leaders at all levels must model entrepreneurial behaviors and mindsets, and to actively support and champion intrapreneurial initiatives within their teams and across the organization. Provide training and coaching to help leaders develop the skills and confidence to foster intrapreneurship and hold them accountable for creating a culture that values and enables innovation at all levels.

Implementing these strategies and creating a supportive and empowering environment for intrapreneurship, serves to engage the full potential of their employees and drive sustainable innovation and growth from within the organization (Wiener, 2023). However, fostering intrapreneurship requires a long-term commitment and a willingness to experiment, learn, and adapt over time. Organizations should continuously assess and refine their approaches based on feedback, results, and changing circumstances, and seek out best practices and lessons learned from other successful intrapreneurial organizations.

CHAPTER 21

Establishing External Partnerships and Open Innovation Practices

"If you have an apple and I have an apple, and we exchange apples then you and I will still each have one apple. But if you have an idea and I have an idea and we exchange these ideas, then each of us will have two ideas."

—George Bernard Shaw

stablishing external partnerships and engaging in open innovation practices can be a powerful way for organizations to access new ideas, technologies, and capabilities, and to accelerate innovation and growth. However, pursuing external partnerships and open innovation can also have implications for an organization's internal emphasis on building its own innovation capabilities. There are potential implications to this approach.

Engaging in external partnerships and open innovation initiatives requires significant time, resources, and attention from leaders and employees. This can potentially divert resources and focus away from internal innovation and scheduled efforts, particularly if the organization has limited bandwidth or competing priorities (Rua, Musiello-Neto and Arias-Oliva, 2023). Organizations need to carefully balance their investments in external and internal innovation and ensure that both are aligned with the overall strategy and goals. Collaborating with external partners or participating in open innovation platforms may require different incentives, rewards, and recognition systems than those used for internal innovation. For example, employees may be more motivated by the opportunity to work with leading experts or brands, or to create impact beyond the boundaries of their own organization. Organizations need to ensure that their incentives and rewards systems are flexible and adaptable enough to accommodate different types of innovation, while still maintaining fairness and consistency.

Engaging in external partnerships and open innovation often requires a different culture and mindset than that of traditional, internally focused innovation. Employees may need to be more open, collaborative, and adaptable when working with external partners, and more willing to share ideas and knowledge beyond the boundaries of their own organization. This can be a significant shift for organizations that have traditionally valued secrecy, control, and ownership over their intellectual property. Leaders need to actively shape and model a culture that values and enables open innovation, while still protecting the organization's core assets and competitive advantages.

To fully realize the benefits of external partnerships and open innovation, organizations need to be able to effectively integrate and leverage the ideas, technologies, and capabilities acquired through these initiatives. This requires strong communication, coordination, and alignment between internal and external innovation teams, as well as the ability to adapt and scale promising ideas and solutions across the organization. Leaders need to create the structures, processes, and culture that enable seamless integration and collaboration between internal and external innovation efforts. External partnerships and open innovation initiatives can often provide quick wins and short-term benefits, such as access to new markets, technologies, or customer insights. However, they may not always contribute to the long-term strategic goals or capabilities of the organization. Leaders need to ensure that external innovation efforts are balanced with investments in internal innovation and capability building, and that they are aligned with the long-term vision and priorities of the organization.

There are risks associated in working with external partners or participating in open innovation platforms can create new challenges and risks related to intellectual property, data security, and competitive intelligence. Organizations need to have clear policies, processes, and agreements in place to manage these risks, and to ensure that they are able to capture and protect the value created through external partnerships and open innovation (Rua, Musiello-Neto and Arias-Oliva, 2023). This may require new skills, expertise, and legal frameworks that are different from those used for internal innovation.

If external partnerships and open innovation initiatives are not managed carefully, they can potentially demotivate or disengage internal employees who may feel that their own ideas and contributions are being overlooked or undervalued. Leaders need to ensure that internal innovation remains a priority and that employees are recognized and rewarded for their contributions, even as the organization pursues external collaboration and open innovation.

To mitigate these potential implications and ensure that external partnerships and open innovation practices enhance rather than detract from internal innovation, organizations should develop a clear and integrated innovation strategy that articulates the role and value of both internal and external innovation, and how they will work together to achieve the organization's goals (Winsor, 2024). This move may be facilitated through the creation of governance structures and processes that enable effective communication, coordination, and decision-making between internal and external innovation teams, and that ensure alignment with the overall organization strategy and priorities. Such governance structures must establish clear policies, processes, and agreements for managing intellectual property, data security, and competitive intelligence in the context of external partnerships and open innovation and ensure that all employees understand and adhere to these guidelines. With these constructs in place, the innovation efforts must be continuously assessed to ensure awareness with the changing environmental conditions, and that it remains aligned with the long-term goals and capabilities of the organization.

Training and support should play a significant role to help employees develop the skills and mindsets needed to effectively engage in external partnerships and open innovation, while still maintaining a strong focus on internal innovation and capability building.

While pursuing external partnerships and open innovation practices can bring significant benefits and opportunities for organizations, it can also have implications for their internal innovation efforts (Winsor, 2024). The existence of a clear and integrated strategy, the creation of effective governance and processes, and the provisioning of training and support leads to a strong culture of innovation. Additionally, by continuously adapting and aligning innovation processes organizations can successfully balance and leverage both internal and external innovation to drive growth and competitiveness (Mention, 2017).

PART V

Measuring and Sustaining Innovation

CHAPTER 22

Developing Measures for Innovation Success

"Not everything that can be counted counts, and not everything that counts can be counted."

—Albert Einstein

Measuring innovation success is paramount for organizations to comprehend the impact and effectiveness of their innovation efforts and make well-informed decisions about resource allocation and continuous improvement. However, measuring innovation can be a challenging task, as it often involves complex, uncertain, and long-term outcomes that may not be easily quantifiable or attributable to specific initiatives (El Bassiti and Aljoun, 2016).

To effectively measure innovation success, organizations can employ a combination of different types of measures, including input, process, output, outcome, and portfolio measures. Input measures focus on the resources and investments an organization puts into innovation, such as R&D spending as a percentage of revenue or allocated budget, the number of employees dedicated to innovation, partnerships or collaborations with external innovation partners, and the number of ideas generated or submitted through innovation channels (Ciric, Borocki, Gracanin and Lalic, 2016). While input measures alone do not guarantee success, they provide a sense of an organization's commitment to and capacity for innovation.

Process measures, on the other hand, focus on the efficiency and effectiveness of an organization's innovation processes. These measures include time from idea generation to realization or commercialization, the number of ideas that progress through each stage of the innovation process, the percentage of projects that meet key milestones or fast failure gates, and feedback and satisfaction scores from innovation participants and stakeholders. Process measures help organizations identify bottlenecks, gaps, or inefficiencies in their innovation processes and make targeted improvements over time (El Bassiti and Aljoun, 2016).

Output measures focus on the tangible results and deliverables of innovation efforts, such as the number of new products, services, or business models launched, the percentage of revenue from new products or services (e.g., vitality index), the number of patents filed or granted, and the number of publications or citations in scientific journals. Output measures provide a clear and measurable way to track the productivity and impact of an organization's innovation efforts and to compare performance against peers or industry benchmarks (Ciric, Borocki, Gracanin and Lalic, 2016).

Outcome measures focus on the broader impact and value that innovation creates for an organization and its stakeholders. These measures include revenue growth or market share gains attributable to innovation, cost savings or efficiency gains from process or business model innovations, improvements in customer satisfaction, loyalty, or lifetime value, and enhancements to brand reputation, employee engagement, or social impact. While outcome measures are often the most meaningful and important indicators of innovation success in meeting the organization's strategic goals, they can also be the most difficult to measure and attribute directly to specific innovation initiatives.

Portfolio measures focus on the overall health and performance of an organization's innovation portfolio across different types, stages, and risk levels of initiatives (Ciric, Borocki, Gracanin and Lalic, 2016). These measures include the balance of incremental, breakthrough, and disruptive innovations, the distribution of resources and investments across different innovation areas and alignment of the innovation portfolio with organizational strategy and goals. Portfolio measures help organizations ensure that they are making smart, balanced, and strategic investments in innovation and managing risk and uncertainty effectively.

While quantitative metrics are important, it is important to monitor the qualitative indicators, as well. The cultural shift is something to monitor as a means of understanding the growth of the organization's innovation culture. In particular, notice the changes in employee behavior and attitudes towards innovation. Another qualitative aspect to focus on is the level of knowledge creation. Is the organization gaining new insights from developed capabilities, even from "failed" projects?

Within the chosen business domain, is the organization gaining external recognition as observed by an increase in Industry awards, media coverage, or competitor responses? In related areas, is the organization noticing an increase in customer enthusiasm? Has there also been increased employee participation in innovation initiatives over time? Additionally, the consideration of factors such as creativity, talent, number of new ideas, and the level of collaboration with customers are intangibles that may make a significant difference in the levels of innovation success of the organization (Ciric, Borocki, Gracanin and Lalic, 2016).

To effectively measure innovation success, organizations should ensure that their measures are aligned with the organization's overall strategy, goals, and values, clearly defined, communicated, and understood by all stakeholders, regularly tracked, reported, and reviewed by leadership and governance bodies, used to inform decision-making, resource allocation, and continuous improvement efforts, benchmarked against relevant peers, competitors, or industry standards, and adjusted and adapted over time as the organization's innovation priorities and capabilities evolve (Lewrick, 2023).

Ultimately, the most effective measures of innovation success will depend on an organization's specific context, goals, and stakeholders (El Bassiti and Aljoun, 2016). Using a range of input, process, output, outcome, and portfolio measures and ensuring that these measures are aligned, actionable, and adaptable organizations can create a robust and meaningful framework for measuring and managing innovation performance over defined periods of time.

While measuring innovation performance can be helpful in managing an organization's ability to meet its strategic goals and remain competitive, the selection of inappropriate measures may work again the goals. An example of such a measure is the Effectiveness Index that looks at the number of innovations produced over time. When organizations reward their respective managers based on volume of products, those managers may begin to select ideas and projects that are low-risk, and thus, easier to successfully produce. As a direct result, the organization develops and behaves as a quantity over quality entity. Note the emphasis on the reward system that promotes this type of outcome. Another factor is the selectivity criteria that allows enables this type of outcome. The bottom line is that the most appropriate innovation measures must align with the goals of the organization and encourage the selection and pursuit of the highest potential ideas and projects that will keep the organization competitive (Ciric, Borocki, Gracanin and Lalic, 2016).

CHAPTER 23

Implementing Continuous Improvement

"Continuous improvement is better than delayed perfection."

—Mark Twain

I mplementing effective continuous improvement processes is essential for organizations to sustain and optimize their innovation activities over time. Continuous improvement involves the ongoing, incremental enhancement of products, services, processes, and capabilities, based on feedback, learning, and best practices. To improve on a continual basis requires clear, measurable goals and metrics for innovation performance, aligned with the organization's overall strategy and priorities (Plenert, 2012).. Organizations need to routinely track and report on these metrics and use them to identify areas for improvement and to set targets for future performance.

Ideally, organizations should develop and implement a data-driven process instead of guessing to determine the organization's innovation progress. The best way to understand the level of improvement through innovation is to collect and analyze data on innovation activities, such as idea generation, project progress, customer feedback, and financial performance. It is a great idea to use tools such as surveys, interviews, focus groups, and analytics to gather insights and identify patterns and trends. Innovators should share and discuss this data with relevant stakeholders to inform decision-making and improvement efforts.

It is a good practice to schedule and hold regular reviews and retrospectives with innovation teams and stakeholders to reflect on successes, challenges, and lessons learned. To standardize the engagements, try using structured formats such as after-action reviews, post-mortem analyses, or agile retrospectives to facilitate open and constructive dialogue. Document and share key insights and action items from these reviews and follow up to ensure that improvements are implemented.

To continue to foster the culture of innovation, regularly emphasize the value of experimentation and iteration, where innovation teams are encouraged to test and refine their ideas and solutions based on feedback and data. Encourage employees to use approaches such as rapid prototyping, minimum viable products, or split testing to quickly validate and improve innovations. Celebrate and learn from both successes and failures and use them to inform future experiments and iterations.

It is fine to learn from others outside of the corporate environment. This includes monitoring the advances of competitors. Look outside the organization to identify best practices, trends, and innovations from other companies, industries, or domains.

Attending conferences, joining innovation networks, or participating in benchmarking studies to stay up to date on the latest
developments and to learn from the experiences of others
(Fonseca, Silva, Silva & Pereira, 2019). Adapt and apply relevant insights and practices to the organization's own innovation
activities.

It is vitally important to continuously encourage collaboration
and knowledge sharing across different innovation teams, functions, and levels of the organization. Innovative organizations must
strive and succeed at creating opportunities for cross-functional
learning and problem-solving, such as innovation communities
of practice, hackathons, or peer coaching programs. To make
tracking of details less arduous, encourage the use of knowledge
management systems, such as wikis, forums, or databases, to
capture and share innovation-related knowledge and best practices (Lee, Yeh, Yu, and Luo, 2023).

To continually elevate the knowledge and skill level of the
workforce, make it a priority to invest in training and development opportunities for innovation teams and leaders, to build their
skills and capabilities in areas such as creativity, design thinking,
lean startup, or agile methodologies. Given that people have different learning modes, think about offering a mix of formal and
informal learning opportunities, such as workshops, e-learning
courses, mentoring, or stretch assignments. Encourage innovation team members to pursue external certifications or degrees
that enhance their expertise and credibility.

While there is a big focus on improving the organization and
its people, remember to proactively engage customers and
other stakeholders in the innovation process, to gather their
feedback, insights, and ideas for improvement. Use techniques

such as customer co-creation, user experience testing, or advisory boards to involve customers in the design and refinement of innovations. Communicate regularly with stakeholders on the progress and impact of innovation activities and seek their input and support for continuous improvement efforts.

As an innovative organization, consider adopting or creating a formal means of innovation management to account for enterprise-wide innovation activities. Such a platform can be crafted to register, track and provide performance information that is tailored for each level within the enterprise. The platform can be used to track and prioritize innovation projects, allocate resources, manage risks, and measure performance. Continuously monitor and optimize these systems based on feedback and results and ensure that they remain aligned with the organization's evolving needs and capabilities. The innovation management platform provides the means of examining all innovation endeavors within the organization. This platform is separate and distinct from the adaptable innovation methodology that the organization selected that defines the innovation process that would be used for innovation pursuits.

As with all the previous suggestions for growing the corporate innovation culture, continue to celebrate and recognize the contributions and achievements of innovation teams and individuals in driving continuous improvement. Use a mix of formal and informal recognition mechanisms, such as awards, bonuses, promotions, or public acknowledgements, to reinforce the value and importance of continuous improvement (Al Darmaki and Ismail, 2019). Share success stories and best practices widely across the organization, to inspire and motivate others to pursue their own improvement efforts.

Continuous improvement processes enable organizations to create an environment that encourages ongoing learning, experimentation, and optimization in their innovation activities (Fonseca, Silva, Silva & Pereira, 2019). They can also ensure that their innovation efforts remain relevant, impactful, and competitive over time, as markets, technologies, and customer needs evolve.

However, it's important to note that continuous improvement is not a one-time event, but an ongoing journey that requires sustained commitment, resources, and leadership support. Organizations should approach continuous improvement as a strategic imperative and embed it into the fabric of their innovation culture and processes.

They should also be prepared to adapt and adjust their continuous improvement approaches based on changing circumstances, feedback, and results. What works well in one context or stage of innovation may not be effective in another, and organizations need to be agile and responsive in their improvement efforts.

Ultimately, the most effective continuous improvement processes for innovation will depend on an organization's specific goals, capabilities, and culture. But by establishing clear goals and metrics, gathering and analyzing data, conducting regular reviews and retrospectives, embracing experimentation and iteration, benchmarking and learning from others, fostering collaboration and knowledge sharing, providing training and development, engaging customers and stakeholders, implementing innovation management systems, and celebrating and recognizing improvements, organizations can create a powerful engine for ongoing innovation (Plenert, 2012).

CHAPTER 24

Ensuring Long-Term Commitment

"The best time to plant a tree was 20 years ago. The second-best time is now."

—Chinese Proverb

Ensuring long-term commitment and resources for innovation is critical for organizations to sustain and scale their innovation efforts over time. Innovation is not a one-time project or initiative, but an ongoing process that requires consistent investment, leadership, and support. Organizations can go about ensuring long-term commitment and resources for innovation in very specific ways.

Given the traditional top-down organization of many of today's organizations, introducing innovation in such environments will be met with skepticism and disdain. The purpose from transforming the organization from its traditional ways to more innovation-driven ways is not easy but necessary. This strategic narrative must be presented to the workforce as an imperative for the organization's ability to compete in its chosen market. The leadership must ensure that innovation is clearly aligned with the organization's overall strategy, goals, and values. Communicate how innovation contributes to the organization's mission, vision, and priorities, and how it creates value for customers, stakeholders, and society. Leadership must embed innovation into the organization's strategic planning, budgeting, and performance management processes, and ensure that it remains a top leadership priority over time. Dedicated funding and resource pools for innovation should be created that are separate from the organization's core operating budgets. This way, there is flexibility in the use of a mix of centralized and decentralized funding models, such as corporate innovation funds, business unit innovation budgets, or venture capital-style investment vehicles, to support different types and stages of innovation. Ensure that funding and resources are sufficient, predictable, and long-term, to enable sustained investment in innovation capabilities and initiatives. Leadership has to exercise care in the manner the communications affect the workforce. Leadership communications occurs verbally and in observable behavior. If the workforce observes that the messaging is more about innovation theatre than actual sincerity, the strategy will likely not succeed (Canic, 2020).

To kickstart innovation within the organization, leaders must be accountable for delivering the message to the workforce and for helping managers and to develop the means to transform the organization at all levels. "Defining innovation broadly means at least three things for senior managers: enriching projects through multiple innovations; paying attention to all the specific processes within innovation; and combining top-down and bottom-up innovation" (Deschamps, 2012). Senior leaders should serve as executive sponsors and champions for innovation. These leaders should have the authority, influence, and resources to drive innovation across the organization, and to remove barriers and obstacles to success. They can establish clear governance structures and processes for innovation, such as innovation councils, steering committees, or advisory boards, to provide oversight, guidance, and accountability for innovation activities.

A typical governance framework may have the characteristics of being risk averse and judge instances of innovative activity through the eyes of traditional business practices. The ese frameworks are rule-driven and count of market stability. Given the fast-paced business and technology environments, that style of thinking and behavior is outmoded and must take into account the modern realities. Organizations, instead, must be able to anticipate and adapt to future realities. They can do so by studying the markets, technologies and state-of-the-art research and overlay their findings on defined problem spaces to identify opportunities that indicate promise (Tõnurist, Hanson, Polchar, Bleckenwegner, and Buisman, 2020).

Companies must invest in building the skills, capabilities, and talent needed to drive innovation over the long term. Provide training, development, and mentoring opportunities for employees to learn and apply innovation methodologies, such as design thinking, lean startup, or agile. Hire and retain diverse talent with innovation expertise and experience and create career paths and incentives for innovation roles and contributions. Foster a culture of learning, experimentation, and risk-taking, where employees feel empowered and motivated to innovate (Canic, 2020).

Collaborate with external partners, such as startups, universities, research institutions, or industry consortia, to access new ideas, technologies, and capabilities for innovation. Participate in open innovation platforms, accelerators, or corporate venturing programs to tap into broader innovation ecosystems and networks (Rua, Musiello-Neto and Arias-Oliva, 2023). Use partnerships and alliances to share costs, risks, and rewards of innovation, and to accelerate and scale innovation efforts beyond the organization's own boundaries.

Regularly communicate and celebrate the progress, achievements, and impacts of innovation across the organization. Share success stories, case studies, and metrics that demonstrate the value and benefits of innovation for customers, employees, and stakeholders. Recognize and reward individuals, teams, and business units that contribute to innovation, and create a culture of pride and enthusiasm for innovation (Al Darmaki and Ismail, 2019). Use internal and external communication channels, such as town halls, newsletters, social media, or investor relations, to build awareness, support, and momentum for innovation.

While assessing the value of innovation within the organization, it is important to link personnel performance as they relate to innovation. One method is to incorporate innovation goals, metrics, and incentives into the organization's performance management and reward systems (Kremer and Williams, 2010). Clear expectations and targets must be detailed for innovation performance at individual, team, and business unit levels, and hold leaders and employees accountable for meeting them. A mix of financial and non-financial incentives can be used, such as bonuses, equity, promotions, or recognition, to motivate and reward innovation contributions and achievements. Ensure that innovation incentives are aligned with the organization's overall strategy and values, and that they encourage both short-term and long-term innovation success (Al Darmaki and Ismail, 2019).

Markets and competitors are continuously changing and that requires regular assessment of processes, tools, knowledge and skills (Lee, Yeh, Yu, and Luo, 2023). Such changes may require modification to the organization's innovation strategies, processes, and capabilities based on changing market, technology, and customer needs. Use a mix of quantitative and qualitative measures, such as innovation metrics, customer feedback, or employee surveys, to evaluate the effectiveness and impact of innovation efforts. Benchmark innovation performance against industry peers and best practices and identify areas for improvement and optimization. Organization's must be willing to pivot, experiment, and learn from failures, and to adjust innovation approaches based on new insights and opportunities (Tõnurist, Hanson, Polchar, Bleckenwegner, and Buisman, 2020).

The people leading the organization's innovation apparatus must actively engage the organization's board of directors, governance boards, investors, and other key stakeholders in supporting and championing innovation. Provide regular updates and presentations on innovation strategies, progress, and results, and seek their input, guidance, and advocacy. Stakeholders must be educated on the importance and value of innovation for the organization's long-term competitiveness and growth and build their confidence and trust in the organization's innovation capabilities and leadership.

Ultimately, ensuring long-term commitment and resources for innovation requires embedding innovation into the organization's culture, values, and DNA (Coffman, 2006). This means creating an environment where innovation is not just a project or initiative, but a way of thinking, working, and behaving across the organization. Leaders and employees at all levels should be encouraged and empowered to innovate, and to challenge the status quo in pursuit of new and better ways of creating value. Innovation should be celebrated as a core part of the organization's identity and purpose, and as a key driver of its long-term success and impact. Implementing these approaches can create the necessary foundations, structures, and cultures to sustain and scale innovation over the long term. However, it's important to recognize that ensuring long-term commitment and resources for innovation is not a one-time or easy task, but an ongoing journey that requires persistent effort, adaptation, and leadership.

Organizations should approach innovation as a strategic imperative and invest in it with the same level of focus, discipline, and resources as they do for other critical business functions, such as finance, marketing, or operations. They should also be prepared to face challenges, setbacks, and resistances along the way, and to learn and adapt their innovation approaches based on changing circumstances and feedback.

Ultimately, the most successful and innovative organizations are those that have a deep and enduring commitment to innovation as a core part of their DNA, and that continuously invest in the people, processes, and cultures needed to drive innovation and growth over the long haul (Coffman, 2006). Using the approaches outlined above, organizations can position themselves to join the ranks of these innovation leaders, and to create lasting value and impact for their customers, employees, and society.

CHAPTER 25

Technologies to Enable and Accelerate Innovation

"Any sufficiently advanced technology is indistinguishable from magic."

—Arthur C. Clarke

While the focus is on transforming traditional organizations into innovation powerhouses by changing the mindset and culture of its people, there is an opportunity, however, to discuss how both themes may be accelerated to achieve the organizational goals. This is by applying the appropriate technology and processes to build the reinforcement systems into the organization by the establishment of technology that implements the ideas and the processes to standardize the desired actions and behaviors that help to transform the organization.

Many of the current and past innovation sources tout the virtues of various popular innovation methodologies and the detailed processes used to approach pain points in unique and practical ways. These are the types of innovation outcomes sought to solve problems that customers would be happy to purchase. When examining the innovation methodologies, however, the expectation conjured in the mind of many people is that of whiteboards, easels, fruit-scented markers and scotch tape. All these concrete hints scream manual, human-centric and human-driven processes.

While these manual processes serve to educate the participating innovators on the processes and in many cases lead to a desired outcome, manual processes do not scale. Recall that a goal of innovation is to be competitive in the company's chosen market. That recognition requires the production of novel, practical and desirable products that meet the demands of a continuously changing market. To achieve this goal, a means of converting the manual processes into automation-assisted innovation processes is required.

While some tools exist to address automating innovation processes, the largest collection of them fall into the idea management category. Idea management is common to all modern innovation methodologies. While it offers needed functionality, it is not the complete set of functionalities to move ideas from their respective nascent states to the point where they are converted to an adopted innovation.

Instrumenting all facets of an innovation methodology's process can be an overwhelming undertaking using traditional software development approaches. Processes change routinely and while software-based systems are fairly robust, many cannot change at the rate that the market demands. A dominant part of the reason is the knowledge required by developers of such systems. Developers would be challenged to augment function-ality within the innovation system, and this may introduce risks to the businesses meeting their goals.

One of the more promising technologies that emerged over the last few years has been that of Generative Artificial Intelligence (Gen-AI) and it may address many of the issues men-tioned concerning the traditional software development process. AI technologies represent a shift toward training models to rec-ognize patterns and to communicate with users in their native communications modes. In short, system users can engage AI systems using voice and text and it responds in kind. The AI system has a base-level training when initially unveiled but it grows in "intelligence" as it learns via user interactions (Metzl, 2024). Such technologies represent a game changing set of opportunities to help the innovation community realize its strategic goals and to establish and maintain competitiveness over the long-term.

AI is revolutionizing various aspects of the innovation process (Metzl, 2024).. The process of innovating is no longer a tedious process. Nearly every facet of the process can benefit from AI-based technologies. Idea Generation, for instance, can engage generative AI chatbots to generate novel concepts and com-binations (Papagiannis, 2017). Machine learning algorithms can be used to identify emerging patterns and trends in the market. If innovators need to assess the originality or the potential of their respective innovation ideas, AI-enabled tools can rapidly and accurately analyze patent databases to assess novelty and potential opportunities. AI can also offer great benefits in inno-vation prototyping. AI-based design software, for example, can create optimized product designs based on design parameters and constraints. Additionally, organizations can gain benefits from

AI analysis of customer insights. This capability could be enabled using Natural Language Processing (NLP) analysis of customer feedback at scale to inform future product and service designs. In the present day, for instance, AI-based avatars are being used to provide product descriptions in Internet ads, answer calls and help troubleshoot cable television issues with customers. The dynamic creation of avatars to engage innovators in intellectual brainstorming sessions about the features and faults of proposed ideas is entirely within the realm of possibilities.

While AI can accelerate and enhance innovation processes, human creativity, empathy, and strategic thinking remain crucial for breakthrough innovations.

Depending on the level of involvement in organizational innovation, technology may be necessary also to help organize information and innovation pursuits that may be initiated throughout the organization.

Keep in mind that many organizations that are new to innovation practices may make the mistake of thinking that idea capture and management automation is the only facet of innovation that requires a technology assist. That idea is flawed because it does not account for follow-on activities and outcomes that may result from the selection of an idea the organization chooses to pursue.

Once the entire innovation process is designed for the organization, any enabling technology must be designed to assist innovators from the beginning of the process to the end of the process. This is critical because if an idea flames out of the process, the organization will need to capture the knowledge that caused it not to be successful.

Are there existing tools on the commercial market to enable organizational innovation? This is an excellent question, and the answer is both yes and no. Tools that support some portion of well-known innovation methods are available on the market. While many are project management tools that are recast as innovation tools, they do offer some value, but each organization is different and may require customizations that these tools typically do not support.

Given start-up schedules and funding issues, an organization may start with office automation tooling, such as the Microsoft or Google office suites, respectively. Most organizations, however, will quickly outgrow these solutions and require some more robust that can service the entire enterprise and is customizable to meet the specific needs of the organization.

CHAPTER 26

Conclusion and Further Explorations

"The future belongs to those who believe in the beauty of their dreams."

—Eleanor Roosevelt

In conclusion, transforming organizations through people and culture is a critical imperative for driving innovation and long-term success in today's rapidly changing business environment. Throughout this discussion, a range of ideas have been explored with key insights and strategies for building a culture of innovation. While some of the included information touched on setting up the environments to host and manage innovation effectively, the real emphasis was intentionally placed on growing the people in ways that encourage, reward and strengthen them and the organizations for which they work. This type of growth was not limited to the people at the bottom of the traditional organizational hierarchy. It

necessarily included people serving at all levels of the organization. The mindset changes are required whether the "organization"
exists as a for-profit company, non-profit company, government
agency, military element or academic institution, there is value in
all the participants. Taking on the suggested shifts in the mindset
can help the organization make the proper adjustments to grow
the innovation culture.

Fostering an innovation mindset and rethinking the concept
of failure is essential, as is aligning organizational values, policies,
and practices with innovation. Identifying and developing innovation advocates, sponsors, and different types of champions, while
providing innovation training and skill development opportunities, can help to embed innovation throughout the organization.
Encouraging and incentivizing cross-functional collaboration and
knowledge sharing, implementing effective idea generation and
evaluation processes, and recognizing and rewarding innovative
contributions are all important elements of a culture of innovation.

Supporting employee well-being and work-life balance, evaluating and optimizing organizational structures for innovation,
and balancing centralized and decentralized decision-making
in innovation governance are also key considerations. Fostering
internal entrepreneurship and intrapreneurship, establishing external partnerships and open innovation practices, measuring and
sustaining innovation through effective metrics and processes,
implementing continuous improvement processes for innovation
activities, and ensuring long-term commitment and resources for
innovation are all critical strategies for driving innovation forward.

Implementing these strategies requires a holistic and
persistent effort that engages employees at all levels of the organization, from senior leaders to front-line innovators. It involves

creating an environment that supports and celebrates curiosity, creativity, experimentation, and collaboration, and that provides the resources, tools, and incentives needed to turn ideas into impact. However, building a culture of innovation is an ongoing journey that requires sustained commitment, leadership, and investment over time. Organizations will inevitably face challenges, setbacks, and resistances along the way, and will need to adapt and evolve their approaches based on changing circumstances and feedback.

As companies mature in their respective understanding of innovation methodologies and practices, so will the selection and implementation of the most appropriate measures to assess the effectiveness of the holistic innovation approach adopted by the organization. Measures are a great way to assess innovation in quantifiable terms but there are intangibles as well and they are, in some cases, more important than the hard numbers. What are the attitudes and perspectives of the workforce and their aggregate rationale for participating or avoiding corporate innovation? Is there trust established with company leadership that values the employee, or do they believe the humans are likely to be phased out over time as new technologies like AI begin to play larger roles?

Embracing the insights and strategies outlined in this discussion and engaging employees at all levels as active champions and drivers of innovation, organizations can position themselves for long-term success and impact in an increasingly complex and dynamic world. They can tap into the full potential of their people and culture to create new sources of value, growth, and competitiveness, and to make a positive difference for their customers, communities, and society as a whole.

The call to action for readers is clear: champion innovation within your own organizations and be a catalyst for the kind of transformative change that can unlock new possibilities and create a better future for all. Whether you are a senior leader setting the strategic direction for innovation, a manager empowering and developing your team's innovation capabilities, or an individual contributor bringing your unique skills and ideas to the table, you have a vital role to play in driving innovation forward.

The pervasive mindset of curiosity, courage, and collaboration are key to putting the insights and strategies from this discussion into practice. Leaders can help to build a culture of innovation that engages and inspires everyone in your organization to be their best and do their best work. Being a leader and a role model for the kind of innovation that creates value not just for the organization, but for the wider world. The future of innovation starts with each person, and the time to act is now.

References

Achdiat, Mulyani, Azis, & Sukmadilaga. (2023). Roles of organizational learning culture in promoting innovation. The Learning Organization, 30(1), 76-92.

Al Darmaki, S. J., Omar, R., & Ismail, W. K. W. (2019). Driving innovation: Reviewing the role of rewards. Journal of Human Resource and Sustainability Studies, 7, 406-415. https://doi.org/10.4236/jhrss.2019.73027

Alves, M. F. R., & Galina, S. V. R. (2018). Literature on organizational innovation: Past and future. Innovation & Management Review, 15(1), 2-19.

Association of American Universities. (2019, February). Employer-provided educational assistance benefits. www.aau.edu

Azizi, M., Hosseinloo, H., Maley, J. F., & Dabić, M. (2023). Entrepreneurial coaching for innovation in SMEs: Development and validation of a measurement scale. European Journal of Innovation Management, 26(7), 696-714. https://doi.org/10.1108/EJIM-07-2023-0546

Barhydt, J. (2023). Psychological safety in startup organizations [Master's thesis, Pepperdine University].

Battye, G. (2024). The authentic organization: How to create a psychologically safe workplace. John Wiley & Sons.

Bello, B. G., Tula, S. T., Omotoye, G. B., Kess-Momoh, A. J., & Daraojimba, A. I. (2024). Work-life balance and its impact in modern organizations: An HR review. World Journal of Advanced Research and Reviews.

Biuk-Aghai, R. P., & Hawryszkiewycz, I. T. (1999). Analysis of virtual workspaces. In Proceedings of the 1999 International Symposium on Database Applications in Non-Traditional Environments.

Brown, J. (2022). How to be an inclusive leader: Your role in creating cultures of belonging where everyone can thrive (2nd ed.). Berrett-Koehler Publishers.

Canic, M. (2020). Ruthless consistency: How committed leaders execute strategy, implement change, and build organizations that win. McGraw Hill.

Catmull, E. (2014). Creativity, Inc. Random House.

Ciric, D., Borocki, J., Gracanin, D., & Lalic, B. (2016). Methodologies for measuring innovation performances. In Proceedings of the 7th International Conference on Mass Customization and Personalization in Central Europe.

Coffman, B. (2006). Building the innovation culture: Some notes on adaptation and change in network-centric organizations. Innovation Labs.

Defense Innovation Board. (2024). Lowering the barriers to innovation. U.S. Department of Defense.

DeGraff, J. (2020). The creative mindset: Mastering the six skills that empower innovation. Berrett-Koehler Publishers.

Deschamps, J. P. (2012). What is innovation governance? IMD. www.imd.org

Desouza, K. C. (2011). Intrapreneurship: Managing ideas within your organization. Rotman-UTP Publishing.

DiJulius, J. R., & Murray, D. D. (2024). The employee experience revolution: Increase morale, retain your workforce, and drive business growth. Greenleaf Book Group.

Dweck, C. (2006). Mindset: The new psychology of success. Random House.

Dyer, J. (2019). The innovator's DNA (Rev. ed.). Harvard Business Review Press.

Edmondson, A. C. (2018). The fearless organization: Creating psychological safety in the workplace for learning, innovation, and growth. Wiley.

El Bassiti, L., & Aljoun, R. (2016). Towards innovation excellence: Why and how to measure innovation performance? In Proceedings of the 2016 6th International Conference on Information and Communication Technology for The Muslim World.

Esposito, P. (2023). The structure of success: A framework to help build your business better. An Inc.

Fonseca, L. R. D., Silva, M. R., Silva, S. W., & Pereira, G. M. (2019). Continuous-learning work environment: A study with developers in software development organizations. Knowledge Management & E-Learning, 11(3), 281-303. https://doi.org/10.34105/j.kmel.2019.11.015

Forbes Insights. (2011). Fostering innovation through a diverse workforce. Global Diversity and Inclusion. www.forbes.com/forbesinsights

Fouejieu, L. (2023). Agile value-driven culture: To be agile or not to be fragile [Doctoral dissertation, Cabrini University].

Friedman, D. J. (2022). Fundamentally different. Independent Publisher.

Gardner, H. K. (2017). Smart collaboration: How professionals and their firms succeed by breaking down silos. Harvard Business Press.

Gerlach, S., & Brem, A. (2018). Idea management revisited: A review of the literature and guide for implementation. International Journal of Innovation Studies, 1(2), 144-161. https://doi.org/10.1016/j.ijis.2017.10.004

REFERENCES

Grivas, C., & Puccio, G. (2011). The innovative team: Unleashing creative potential for breakthrough results. Jossey-Bass.

Gunaratne, K. A. (2001). Internal marketing: An innovative strategic approach to sustainable competitive advantage. UNITEC Institute of Technology.

Gump, L. K. (2024). The inside innovator: A practical guide to intrapreneurship. Fast Company Press.

Hattori, R. A., & Wycoff, J. (2004). Innovation training. ASTD Press.

Heffernan, M. (2015). Beyond measure: The big impact of small changes. Simon & Schuster/Ted.

Herold, C. (2020). Vivid vision: A remarkable tool for aligning your business around a shared vision of the future. Lioncrest Publishing.

Horth, D. M., & Mitchell, M. (2024, February 11). How to foster an innovative mindset at your organization. Center for Creative Leadership.

Howell, J. M., & Higgins, C. A. (1990). Champions of technological innovation. Administrative Science Quarterly.

Hughes, J., Chapnick, D., Block, I., & Saptak, R. (2021, September 26). What is customer-centricity and why does it matter? California Management Review.

Human Resource Management International Digest. (2022). Enhancing employee creativity: Managerial coaching and an innovation climate help creative performance. Human Resource Management International Digest, 30(4), 44–46. https://doi.org/10.1108/HRMID-05-2022-0074

IBM Corporation. (2016). IBM-design-thinking-field-guide-v3.4. IBM.

Intuit. (2019). Design for delight playbook: A guide for everyday innovation. Intuit Education.

Isaksen, S. (2010). Creative approaches to problem solving: A framework for innovation and change (3rd ed.). SAGE Publications.

Ivanova, S., Lee, J., & Jane, K. (2024). Iterative design: A cyclical process of design, testing, and refinement.

Jana, T., & Baran, M. (2023). Subtle acts of exclusion: How to understand, identify, and stop microaggressions (2nd ed.). Berrett-Koehler Publishers.

Jantz, R. C. (2012). A framework for studying organizational innovation in research libraries.

Jassawalla, A., & Sashittal, H. (2006). Collaboration in cross-functional product innovation teams. Advances in Interdisciplinary Studies of Work Teams, 12, 1–25. https://doi.org/10.1016/S1572-0977(06)12001-4

Jia, P., & Xia, Q. (2008). Knowledge management, collaboration and innovation. In International Seminar on Future Information Technology and Management Engineering.

Kahn, W. A. (1990). Psychological conditions of personal engagement and disengagement at work. Academy of Management Journal, 33(4), 692–724. https://doi.org/10.2307/256287

Kamasak, R. (2015). Determinants of innovation performance: A resource-based study. In World Conference on Technology, Innovation and Entrepreneurship.

Katz, B., Du Preez, N., & Schutte, C. (2011). Alignment of a functional innovation strategy. In ISEM 2011 Proceedings (pp. 148–4).

Keko, E., Prevo, G. J., & Stremersch, S. (2017). The what, who and how of innovation generation. In Handbook of research on new product development.

Kremer, M., & Williams, H. (n.d.). Incentivizing innovation: Adding to the tool kit. Harvard University, Brookings Institution, Center for Global Development, and NBER.

Kuratko, D. F., Goldsby, M., & Hornsby, J. (2023). Corporate innovation: Disruptive thinking for organizational success. Wiley.

Lewrick, M. (2023). Design thinking and innovation metrics: Powerful tools to manage creativity, OKRs, product, and business success. Wiley.

Liu, Q., Zhao, X., & Sun, B. (2018). Value co-creation mechanisms of enterprises and users under crowdsource-based open innovation. International Journal of Crowd Science, 2(1), 2–17. https://doi.org/10.1108/IJCS-01-2018-0001

Liu, S., Jiang, W., & Yi, S. (2019). Digging deep into the enterprise innovation ecosystem: How do enterprises build and coordinate innovation ecosystem at firm level. Chinese Management Studies, 13(4), 820–839. https://doi.org/10.1108/CMS-05-2018-0505

Luca, M., & Bazerman, M. H. (2021). The power of experiments: Decision making in a data-driven world. MIT Press.

Maples Jr., M., & Ziebelman, P. (2024). Pattern breakers: Why some start-ups change the future. Public Affairs.

Marchand, L. (2022). The innovation mindset: Eight essential steps to transform any industry. Columbia Business School Publishing.

McKinney, P. (2023). Collaboration is the new competition: Why the future of work rewards a cross-pollinating hive mind & how not to get left behind. Lioncrest Publishing.

Mention, A. L., & Salampasi, D. (2017). Open innovation: Unveiling the power of the human element. World Scientific Publishing Company.

Metzl, J. (2024). Superconvergence: How the genetics, biotech, and AI revolutions will transform our lives, work, and world. Timber Press.

Michaelis, T. L., & Markham, S. K. (2017). Innovation training makes innovation a core competency. Industrial Research Institute.

Misra, S. (2024). Measuring innovation: Perspectives from engineering education and clean energy [Doctoral dissertation, University of Washington].

Möllmann, J. (2023). More than a handshake: Knowledge transfer in structured corporate-startup collaboration programs. Journal of Knowledge Management, 27(10), 2604-2624. https://doi.org/10.1108/JKM-03-2022-0222

Morehead, K. (2022). Enhancing creativity in organizational teams: Development of The Spark Program [Master's project, Buffalo State University]. Digital Commons. https://digitalcommons.buffalostate.edu/creativeprojects/343

Nijhawan, N. (2020). The productive virtual workspace: Making remote working efficient & sustainable. Independent Publisher.

Nimergood, J. (2014). Intrapreneurship: Changing business culture from the inside out. CreateSpace.

Nooraie, M. (2014). The roles of decentralization of the decision-making process between contextual factors and decision process output. International Review of Management and Business Research, 3(1).

Olson, H. H., & Bosch, J. (2016). Collaborative innovation: A model for selecting the optimal ecosystem innovation strategy. In 42nd Euromicro Conference on Software Engineering and Advanced Applications.

Opoku, P., & Duah, H. K. (2019). Relationship among reward systems, knowledge sharing and innovation performance. European Journal of Research and Reflection in Management Sciences, 7(1).

Ozkan, N. N. (2015). An example of open innovation: P&G. In World Conference on Technology, Innovation and Entrepreneurship. Elsevier.

Papagiannis, H. (2017). Augmented human: How technology is shaping the new reality. O'Reilly Media.

Pietersen, W. (2010). Strategic learning: How to be smarter than your competition and turn key insights into competitive advantage. Wiley.

Pinar, C., Storme, M., Davila, A., & Myszkowski, N. (2016). Work-related curiosity positively predicts worker innovation. Journal of Management Development, 35(9).

Plenert, G. (2012). Strategies continuous process improvement (12th ed.). McGraw-Hill.

Puspitasari, S. D., Atmojo, I. R. W., & Daryanto, J. (2024, January 1). Improving experimentation skills through the implementation of project-based learning: Analysis of creative thinking skills. In Mini International Conference of Educational Research and Innovation.

Ramírez, M. A. N., Rivero, B., Ozuna, A. G., Álvarez, R. I. C., & Ramírez, V. C. L. (2017). Relationship between flexible organizational culture and innovation capabilities: The moderating effect of rigid organizational culture. International Review of Management and Marketing.

Ratnaningtyas, D. I., & Wilujeng, I. (2021). Pengembangan perangkat pembelajaran fisika dengan pendekatan saintifik untuk meningkatkan soft skills dan hard skills peserta didik SMA. JPFT (Jurnal Pendidikan Fisika Tadulako Online), 9(1). http://jurnal.untad. ac.id/jurnal/index.php/EPFT/article/view/19294

Rattner, D. M. (2019). My creative space: How to design your home to stimulate ideas and spark innovation. Skyhorse.

Robinson, A. G., & Schroeder, D. M. (2020). The idea-driven organization: Unlocking the power in bottom-up ideas. Berrett-Koehler Publishers.

Rogers, E. M. (2003). Diffusion of innovations (5th ed.). Free Press.

Rua, O. L., Musiello-Neto, F., & Arias-Oliva, M. (2023). Linking open innovation and competitive advantage: The roles of corporate risk management and organisational strategy. Baltic Journal of Management, 18(1).

Sandström, C., & Björk, J. (2009). Idea management systems for a changing innovation landscape. International Journal of Product Development.

Schneeweiss, C. (2010). Decision-making & problem solving, operations research, production & operations management. Springer.

Senge, P. (2006). The fifth discipline: The art and practice of the learning organization (2nd ed.). Random House Business.

Sergeeva, N. (2016). What makes an 'innovation champion'? European Journal of Innovation Management, 19(1), 72–89. https://doi.org/10.1108/SD-02-2016-0029

Sloane, P. (2007). The innovative leader: How to inspire your team and drive creativity. Kogan Page.

Song, J., Yang, Z., Zhang, Z., & Huang, Q. (2020). The correlation analysis between organizational justice, knowledge-hiding behavior and nurses' innovation ability: A cross-sectional study. Wiley.

Stavros, J., & Torres, C. (2021). Conversations worth having: Using appreciative inquiry to fuel productive and meaningful engagement (2nd ed.). Berrett-Koehler Publishers.

Sultana, R., Christ, A., & Meyrueis, P. (2013). Diversity of devices along with diversity of data formats as a new challenge in global teaching and learning system.

Sun, C., & Wei, J. (2019). Digging deep into the enterprise innovation ecosystem: How do enterprises build and coordinate innovation ecosystem at firm level. Chinese Management Studies, 13(4), 820–839. https://doi.org/10.1108/CMS-05-2018-0505

Sunny, D. (2024). Grow creative mindset: Generate ideas on demand, innovate with imagination, spark creativity, and actualize your inner idealist for excellence. Independent Publisher.

Teichert, J. (2023). Boom! Leadership that breaks barriers, challenges convention, and ignites innovation. Capital Leadership Books.

Thackston, J. (2014). Creating a culture of curiosity: Three essentials for leading innovation in your organization. SOAR Performance Group.

Thomke, S. (2001, February). Enlightened experimentation: The new imperative for innovation. Harvard Business Review.

Thomke, S. (2003). Experimentation matters: Unlocking the potential of new technologies for innovation. Harvard Business Review Press.

Tõnurist, P., Hanson, A., Polchar, J., Bleckenwegner, C., & Buisman, H. (2020). Anticipatory innovation governance: What it is, how it works, and why we need it more than ever before. OECD. oecd-opsi.org

Wale, H. (2024). Centralization vs. decentralization: Making effective organizational design decisions. Corporate Finance Institute. https://corporatefinanceinstitute.com/resources/management/centralization/

Wiener, J. (2023). An examination of the relationship between the organizational culture and entrepreneurial orientation in Texas-based small businesses [Doctoral dissertation].

Winsor, J., & Paik, J. H. (2024). Open talent: Leveraging the global workforce to solve your biggest challenges. Harvard Business Review Press.

World at Work. (2022, April). Driving innovation with rewards. World at Work – Total Rewards Association.

Yang, Y. C., & Hsu, J. M. (2010). Organizational process alignment, culture and innovation. African Journal of Business Management, 4(11), 2231-2240.